UK Social Issues

(Second Edition)

George Clarke

Frank Cooney

Irene Morrison

Pulse Publications

Contents

ACKNOWLEDGEMENTS

The authors and publishers would like to thank the following for permission to reproduce copyright material: Empics for photographs on pages 12, 22, 36, 42, 52, 54, 56, 82, 85, 89, 91, 101 ; Reuters/ Toby Melville page 70; Stuart Wright page 75.

Published and typeset by
Pulse Publications
Braehead, Stewarton Road,
by Kilmaurs, Ayrshire
KA3 2NH

Printed and bound by
Thomson Colour Printers

British Library Cataloguing-in-Publication Data
A Catalogue record for this book is available from the British Library

ISBN 0 948 766 05 0
© Clarke, Cooney & Morrison 2006

Chapter 1

Social class in Britain

This chapter examines the ways in which social class is measured, the ways that wealth and poverty are measured and the difference between absolute and relative poverty. These terms will not be specifically examined, but it is important to understand them as they are used throughout the book.

WHAT IS SOCIAL CLASS?

Social class measures economic factors such as wealth, income and occupation; political factors such as status and power; and cultural factors such as lifestyle, values, beliefs, levels of education etc. This is very complex so to make it more manageable occupation is normally used.

Occupation is important and influences other factors such as status, income, wealth and lifestyle. These in turn will be influenced by values and beliefs which vary from person to person. Therefore social class it is not a precise instrument and only broad generalisations may be made.

Why try to define social class?

Planners and researchers in academic, business and government organisations need to be able to analyse the population to understand how it is changing in order to plan for the future. Researchers want to discover and explain why people do the things they do. Businesses want to develop products which will sell so need to know how demand might change. Governments need to plan services and improve the lifestyle and life

chances of the population. Therefore the main purposes of defining class are for research, for predicting and for social engineering.

Ways of defining social class

Attempts have been made to define social class over the past 150 years, ever since people began trying to apply scientific method to the study and understanding of society.

Towards the end of the nineteenth century the UK government was taking increasing responsibility for social matters such as health and education. It needed to be able to quantify the impact of the changes it had introduced. In 1911 the Registrar General introduced a social class model to enable his department to analyse aspects of life in Britain in order to provide information for the government.

The Registrar General's Model of Social Class (RGSC) was used by UK governments from 1911 to 1980. Society was divided into six categories according to occupation. Occupations were ranked by 'their standing in the community' relative to each other.

A Professional etc. occupations
B Managerial and Technical occupations
C1 Non-manual skilled occupations
C2 Manual skilled occupations
D Partly skilled occupations
E Unskilled occupations

It was simple to understand and apply and it enabled government statisticians to compare health

KARL MARX

Historically, the first systematic attempts to define class were by Karl Marx and Max Weber. Karl Marx (1818–63) was a German philosopher who argued that class was solely due to a person's relationship to the means of production. Max Weber (1864–1920) was also German and was the founder of modern sociology. He believed that class is created at a point in time by the demand for the skills that people have in addition to the property they own.

between different groups, provide analysis of employment and unemployment, and investigate poverty and family life across time. The results enabled governments to target resources for social planning.

However, because classification was based on a person's occupation, it omitted large sections of the population such as those who were retired and the unemployed. It also left out wives or husbands who were unemployed and those groups whose incomes came from rents or investments. Another problem was that the categories were too broad. For example, a farmer could be a poor smallholder or a millionaire gentleman farmer.

In response to these shortcomings, government statisticians introduced a new model called the Standard Occupation Classification (SOC) in 1980. It replaced the RGSC and lasted until 2001. It had nine major categories which were further subdivided.

SOC Major categories

1 Managers and Senior Officials
2 Professional Occupations
3 Associate Professional and Technical Occupations
4 Administrative and Secretarial Occupations
5 Skilled Trades Occupations
6 Personal Service Occupations
7 Sales and Customer Service Occupations
8 Process, Plant and Machine Operatives
9 Elementary Occupations

The SOC groups were selected more objectively than the RGSC and therefore were more logical. Occupations were ranked according to the level of skill and the qualifications needed to do the job, so the SOC was more objective than the RGSC. However, it suffered many of the weaknesses associated with the RGSC.

In 2001, the Office for National Statistics introduced the National Statistics Socio-economic Classification which it uses for all official statistics and surveys. The NS-SeC is based on occupation but designed to provide coverage of the whole adult population.

The NS-SeC is more detailed than the SOC. A person's NS-SeC position (their 'class') depends upon the combination of their job and their employment status—in other words whether they are an employer, self-

The National Statistics Socio-economic Classification

1   **Higher managerial and professional occupations**
   1.1   Large employers and higher managerial occupations: company directors, senior managers, senior civil servants, senior police officers
   1.2   Higher professional occupations: doctors, lawyers, teachers and social workers

2   **Lower managerial and professional occupations:** nurses, journalists, actors, musicians, lower ranks in the police and armed forces

3   **Intermediate occupations:** clerks, secretaries, driving instructors, telephone fitters

4   **Small employers and own account workers:** publicans, farmers window cleaners, painters and decorators

5   **Lower supervisory and technical occupations:** printers, plumbers, TV engineers, butchers

6   **Semi-routine occupations:** shop assistants, hairdressers, bus drivers, cooks

7   **Routine occupations:** couriers, labourers, waiters, refuse collectors

8   **Never worked and long-term unemployed:** non-working spouses, unemployed for various reasons

   'Not classified' is added to cover students and other groups

Table 1.1 Source: Office for National Statistics

employed, a manager, a supervisor or an employee. Thus, for example, a baker with twenty five employees would be in a different class from a self-employed baker. In turn, those two would be in different classes from an employee baker who would be in a different class from a baker manager who in turn would be in a different class from a supervisor of bakers. Despite the fact that this is an improvement on previous clas-

sification systems it is still heavily based on occupation.

There are two prominent methods of defining social class currently used by sociologists—Hutton's 30-30-40 Society and the Runciman Scale. Hutton says that the economies of modern industrial societies have created a labour market which divides people into three categories. There are the advantaged who are in full-time, well-paid and secure employment. At the bottom are the disadvantaged who suffer unemployment and are excluded. Between the two is a group of people whose employment is insecure and who are striving to become advantaged but who are more likely to become disadvantaged.

The Runciman Scale is based around economic power, ownership and control, and status based on a person's marketability. If a person owns a company they have economic power. If a person has the power to direct others in the workplace then they have economic power. If a person possesses skills that are prized by society then they have economic power.

HUTTON'S 30-30-40 SOCIETY

	Social Class	Group Characteristics
1	*The Advantaged (top 40%)*	● full-time / self-employed – 2 years in the job ● part-time – 5 years in the job ● strong, effective professional associations or trade unions ● range of work-related benefits ● mainly male workers
2	*The Insecure (middle 30%)*	● part-time / casual workers ● declining employment protection / few benefits ● large number of female workers ● self-employed (especially manual workers) ● fixed-term contract workers
3	*The Disadvantaged (bottom 30%)*	● unemployed (particularly long-term) ● families caught in the poverty trap (e.g. single parents) ● people on government employment schemes ● casual part-time workers

Table 1.2

THE RUNCIMAN SCALE

	Social Class	Examples of Occupation and Status
UPPER CLASS		
1	*Upper*	Corporate owner, senior management, people with high level marketable skills
2	*Upper middle*	Higher grade professional (doctor, lawyer, chief constable), manager, senior civil servant
MIDDLE CLASS		
3	*Middle middle*	Lower grade professional (teacher, police officer), owner of medium size business
4	*Lower middle*	Routine white collar (clerk etc.)
5	*Skilled working*	Electrician, plumber, skilled self-employed
WORKING CLASS		
6	*Unskilled working*	Shop assistant, check-out operator
UNDERCLASS		
7	*Underclass*	Long-term unemployed and benefit dependent

Table 1.3

Does Class exist in the twenty first century?

Social class divisions are far less clear and much less rigid than they were even fifty years ago. However, the evidence indicates that wide variations remain in terms of living standards, the quality of life and life chances. In the recent past, the incomes, wealth and living standards of people in higher occupational classes have increased faster than those of people lower down. For example, a child born in the poorest constituency in Scotland is three times more likely to be born into a workless household and to depend on benefits, is twice as likely to have no qualifications and can expect to live fifteen years less than a person in the most well-off constituency.

Children of unskilled manual labourers are four times more likely to die in an accident than the children of professional parents. Their health is generally worse across all indicators, including obesity, and infant mortality rates are higher.

Children born into higher social classes do better in education and have a better chance of getting higher paid jobs. There is some upward mobility and some people do drift downwards, but the overwhelming majority remain within the social group they are born into. For instance, most children of unskilled workers become unskilled workers and most children of professional workers become professional workers themselves. Therefore to an extent social class exists.

Whether we use the term 'social class' or some other description it is possible and useful to place people into categories for the purposes of research. As a means of studying society, identifying trends, targeting resources and understanding the impact of change, the concept of social class is a useful tool. To the extent that it is possible to arrange the population into identifiable groups with measurable differences, it is reasonable to say that social class does exist in the twenty first century.

ABSOLUTE POVERTY AND RELATIVE POVERTY

The most commonly used definition of absolute poverty is taken from a 1995 United Nations statement which said it was "a condition characterised by severe deprivation of basic human needs". It listed those "basic human needs" as a lack of food, safe drinking water, sanitation facilities, health, shelter, education and access to benefits. A person is said to be living in absolute poverty *only* if he or she suffers from being deprived of two or more of the seven basic human needs.

Relative poverty compares the living standards of people in the lowest sections of a population with those in the upper levels. Measuring relative poverty is largely the same as measuring inequality. Therefore, as the distribution of income changes in a society, the scale of relative poverty will be altered. If a society achieves a more equal income distribution, relative poverty will fall.

How do we measure poverty in the UK?

There are three ways that are used to measure poverty in the UK. The main government measure is provided by the Department of Work and Pensions (DWP) in its annual report on Households Below Average Income (HBAI). A second method is to use Income Support levels. Both of these provide a figure as the measure of poverty. Finally, the Poverty and Social Exclusion Survey (PSE Survey)

provides an alternative measure by identifying a range of items that the people of the UK believe to be necessities, then identifying different groups who lack these items.

The HBAI Report identifies poverty as 60% of the median income. Median income is the middle income in a range of all incomes in the UK. It is that income which has 50% of the nation's incomes above it and 50% below it.

Income Support levels are set by Parliament to provide a basic income for people between 16 and 60 who are living on a low income because they are incapable of work due to illness or disability, or they care for a sick or disabled person, or are a lone parent responsible for a child under 16. Income Support is means tested. Regulations approved by Parliament state the levels of income appropriate to various circumstances—age, family size, disabilities, etc. If income is lower than the rates specified then Income Support makes up the difference.

As Income Support levels are set to reflect the income required to meet basic needs, they can be used as a measure of poverty. However, they are set as the consequence of a political agenda so may not accurately reflect poverty levels in the UK as political considerations will influence the levels set.

The PSE Survey was based on methods pioneered by the Breadline Britain series in 1983 and 1990. A cross section of the population were asked to decide which of fifty four items or activities they felt were necessities in modern Britain. Thirty five of these fifty four items were thought necessary by more than 50% of the population.

The items which the public found to be necessary ranged from beds and bedding for everyone (95%) and heating to warm areas of the house (94%) to a dictionary (53%) and an outfit for a social occasion (51%). The PSE survey identified

people as poor if they could not afford two or more of the items on the list. By comparing the results of the 1983 and 1990 studies they could measure the extent to which the level of poverty had changed over time and the changes in the public's perception of necessities.

These three measures of poverty measure different things. The HBAI survey is a statistical calculation based on the range of incomes existing in the UK over a period of time. The Income Support calculation is intended to identify a basic level of income necessary to survive in the UK, but is influenced by political considerations. Finally, the PSE survey measures the level of poverty among various sections of society by using a snapshot of the public's perceptions of what things are necessary for life in modern Britain.

THE EXTENT OF CHANGES IN CLASS STRUCTURE

The economy of the UK went through radical change during the course of the twentieth century. As class structure is based on people's occupations there have been significant changes in class structure in the UK in the last 100 years.

The most significant change has been in the reduction in the number of manual workers from three-quarters of the working population to just over one-third. (See Table 1.4.) These largely correspond to the DE class groups in the RGSC. There has been a matching expansion in the AB groups which include managers, administrators, higher and lower professionals and employers and proprietors whose percentage of the workforce increased from 14.2% in 1911 to 37.6% in 1991. Clerical workers, foremen, supervisors, and sales workers also saw a significant increase over the course of the century.

Table 1.5 shows that this trend has continued since 1991. There has been a slow but steady increase in the number of people in the A, B and C class groups and a reduction in those in classes D and E. The UK continues to have an upwardly mobile class structure but this is slowing down because there are fewer and fewer children whose parents are in lower class groups, so fewer people can move upwards. As the higher social class groups fill up and the UK increasingly becomes a society of limited class divisions, there will be fewer and fewer opportunities for movement.

Another significant change in social class is the number of women who are counted as part of the workforce. In 1900 there were 5 million women workers who accounted for only 29% of the workforce. Therefore most women in the UK were placed in a social class group which was dependent on their husband's status. A century later the number of women workers had increased to 13 million, accounted for 46% of the total workforce and women were categorised in their own right. This means that social class measurements more accurately reflect society because many more people are directly included.

Social mobility in Scotland

In a study, *Moving Up and Down the Social Class Ladder* in Scotland by Cristina Iannelli and Lindsay Paterson, the researchers found that among adults of working age, nearly two-thirds had moved to a different social class to that in which they had been brought up and over two-thirds of these had moved up the social class ladder.

They also found that there was a reduction in upward mobility com-

pared with earlier generations. This reduction was caused by changes in the class structure. There were fewer people born into manual class groups because these groups had contracted so there were fewer people able to move up. A very large number were not mobile because increasing numbers were born into groups at the top of the

class structure and as a result they had nowhere to rise to.

As the economy changes and there are fewer and fewer D and E type occupations and increasing employment opportunities in groups A to C, social mobility will continue to decrease.

OCCUPATIONAL CLASS IN GREAT BRITAIN 1911 – 1991

	PERCENTAGE OF WORKFORCE	
	1911	**1991**
Managers & administrators	3.4	15.1
Higher professions	1.0	5.3
Lower professions	3.1	13.9
Employers and proprietors	6.7	3.3
Clerical workers	4.5	15.4
Foremen, supervisors	1.3	3.8
Sales	5.4	5.6
Manual workers	74.6	37.7

Table 1.4 Source: Duncan Gallie *Skill Change and the Labour Market: Gender, Class and Unemployment*

OCCUPATIONAL STRUCTURE 1991 – 2000
(Percentage of employment)

	1991	**2000**
Managerial/Administrators	14.2	16.2
Professional	9.4	10.9
Associate Professional	8.8	10.4
Clerical	15.9	14.7
Craft and Related	15.2	11.7
Personal Services	9.1	11.0
Sales	7.8	8.2
Operatives	10.0	8.8
Elementary	8.9	7.7

Table 1.5 Source: *Labour Force Survey*, National Statistics Database

Chapter 2

Inequalities in wealth

THE DIFFERENCE BETWEEN INCOME AND WEALTH

Income is money a person receives over a period of time, usually a week, a month or a year. Income comes in a variety of forms such as a wage or salary from employment, interest on savings, profits or dividends from share ownership, or rent from land and property.

Wealth is "the ownership of assets at a particular point in time" (Social Trends 33). It accumulates from income or inheritance and is calculated by adding up the value of property such as vehicles, artwork, and jewellery which a person owns as well as the value of pensions, shares, insurances and cash in banks and building societies.

Measuring a country's wealth

A country's wealth is expressed as GDP per head. A country's GDP is calculated by adding together the value of all the goods and services produced annually. The GDP per head is the total GDP divided by the population of the country.

To make comparisons between countries, figures are usually expressed in US dollars ($US). To overcome the problem of changes in currency values the figures are expressed in Purchasing Power Parity (PPP). In 2005, the UK had a GDP of $1.867 trillion (PPP).

Gross National Product (GNP) is also used as a measure of wealth. GNP is GDP plus the value of income from overseas investments plus the figures for international trade.

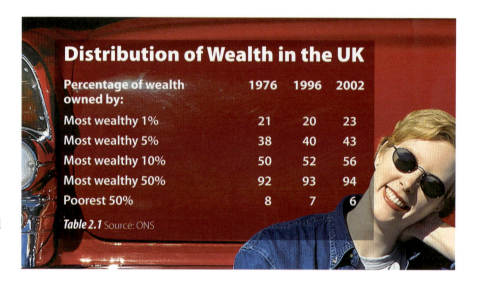

Distribution of Wealth in the UK

Percentage of wealth owned by:	1976	1996	2002
Most wealthy 1%	21	20	23
Most wealthy 5%	38	40	43
Most wealthy 10%	50	52	56
Most wealthy 50%	92	93	94
Poorest 50%	8	7	6

Table 2.1 Source: ONS

How wealthy is the UK?

The UK is an extremely wealthy country. In 2005, the UK's GDP was $1.867 trillion (£1.069 trillion) and its GDP per head was $30,900 (£17,698). The UK ranks eighth in the world for total GDP but twentieth for GDP per head. Countries such as Luxembourg have smaller GDPs than the UK but even smaller populations.

The ownership of **Wealth** in the UK

State pensions 26%
Private pensions 22%
Housing 35%
Savings 17%

Figure 2.1

Pension rights account for nearly half of the wealth of the people in the UK. Home ownership is over one-third of UK wealth, while savings—building society and bank accounts, insurance policies and types of investment such as ISAs—account for around 17%.

However, wealth is not evenly distributed. According to the ONS, in 2002 the wealthiest 1% of the population owned four times the wealth of the bottom 50%. Furthermore, the rich are getting richer while the poor are getting poorer. In the past thirty years the wealthiest groups in society have increased their wealth while the poor have seen their wealth decreasing.

A large proportion of the population have no access to private pensions. For example, half of all lone parents in the UK do not have any access to an occupational pension or a private pension. For a large section of the population state pension rights are their only source of wealth. 30% of families have no savings and 50% of lone parents and young single people have no housing wealth at all.

The ownership of wealth varies throughout a person's lifetime. Most young people have little wealth. They have lower incomes than in later life so cannot save. They may be burdened by debt from student loans and a mortgage. Some face the costs of bringing up a family.

As they get older their mortgages get proportionately smaller as their incomes rise. They start to increase their savings with banks and building societies or they may buy investments. They also gain any inheritance they are likely to get. Their pension rights increase if they have an occupational pension or a private pension.

At the point at which they retire they will be at the maximum extent of their wealth. They have a house which they own and savings and pension rights will be at a maximum. Throughout the rest of their life, savings and pensions will diminish as they are used to maintain their lifestyle. They can pass the residue on to others at their death.

Therefore the majority of the wealth in the UK is owned by those who are around the age of retirement.

Unfortunately, there are large numbers of people who are not in the position to accumulate wealth at any point in their lives. Those who face unemployment, or employment insecurity, those on low wages, many single parent families and the majority of disabled people do not get access to much of the UK's wealth.

WEALTH INEQUALITIES IN BRITAIN

Inequality within a society is measured using the Gini index. A score of zero indicates perfect equality and 100 shows perfect inequality. Using this measure, the UK is one of the least 'equal' societies in the European Union. (See Table 2.2.)

EU **Gini** index scores

Country	Gini index score
Austria	31.0
Belgium	28.7
Czech Republic	25.4
Denmark	24.7
Estonia	37.0
Finland	25.6
France	32.7
Germany	30.0
Greece	35.4
Hungary	24.4
Ireland	35.9
Italy	27.3
Latvia	32.0
Lithuania	34.0
Netherlands	32.6
Poland	31.6
Portugal	35.6
Slovakia	26.3
Slovenia	28.4
Spain	32.5
Sweden	25.0
United Kingdom	36.8
Cyprus, Luxembourg, Malta	No data

Table 2.2
Source: Economic and Social Research Council

The extent of wealth inequality will vary depending on how it is measured.

Extent of poverty according to PSE

According to the PSE 1999 survey, over one-third of the population were classed as poor or vulnerable to poverty. The survey also found that poverty levels had increased. In 1983, 14% of households were classed as poor, a figure which rose to 21% in 1990 and 25.6% in 1999. Therefore, through the 1980s and 1990s, poverty became more widespread.

The survey identified the items that people lacked. 17% of households could not afford to keep their home adequately heated, free from damp or in a decent state of decoration. 13% could not afford essential

Extent of poverty
using the Poverty and Social Exclusion Survey

Poor	25.6%
Vulnerable to poverty	10.3%
Risen out of poverty	1.8%
Not poor	62.2%
Total	100%

Table 2.3
Source: *Poverty and Social Exclusion in Britain* JRF 2000

household goods, like a refrigerator, a telephone or carpets for living areas. 14% did not have enough money to visit friends and family, attend a wedding or a funeral or adequately celebrate a birthday or Christmas.

33% of British children did not get necessities such as three meals a day, toys, out of school activities or adequate clothing. 11% of adults go without essential clothing, such as a 'warm, waterproof coat', because of lack of money and 7% do not have enough money to afford fresh fruit and vegetables, or two meals a day. Over 28% of people in households cannot afford to save or insure their house contents.

Some of the groups most vulnerable to poverty according to the PSE Survey were:
- lone-parent households
- households with no paid workers
- large families
- separated/divorced households
- families with a child under 11
- adults living in one-person households, including single pensioners
- children
- those who left school at 16 or under
- women

These findings are backed up by an analysis of the 2001 census which again illustrated the impact of poverty on lifestyle. For example, income has a big impact on car ownership. As the motor car is the main means of access to supermar-

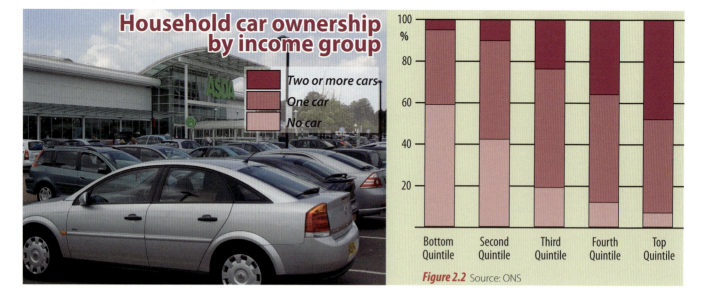

Household car ownership by income group

Legend:
- Two or more cars
- One car
- No car

Categories: Bottom Quintile, Second Quintile, Third Quintile, Fourth Quintile, Top Quintile

Figure 2.2 Source: ONS

ket shopping, visits to friends and relatives, travel to employment and access to entertainment and activities, lack of car ownership can have a major impact on lifestyle and wellbeing. The groups with least access to cars are the elderly (69% with no access) and lone parent families (43%).

Extent of poverty according to HBAI

Measuring poverty using the Households Below Average Income (HBAI) Report sets the poverty line at 60% of median household income, adjusted for household size. (See Chapter 1.) In 2003–04 the poverty level for a two-adult household was £180 per week (after household costs); £100 per week for a single adult; £260 per week for two adults living with two children; and £180 per week for a single adult living with two children.

Using these figures, 11.5 million people in Britain were living in poverty. This represents just over 20% of the population. Although the figure is lower than for the PSE survey it is not too dissimilar. The largest groups facing poverty are 3.5 million children and 2.5 million adults living with them. There are 3.5 million adults of working age who have no dependent children and 2 million pensioners who live in poverty.

Using the calculations for HBAI, Table 2.4 shows that nearly one

million people in Scotland were living in poverty in 2003–04. This is 20% of the population. The level for the whole of the UK is very similar. In 2003 there were just under 1 in 4 people in the UK living in poverty. That is 12.4 million people. The figure includes nearly one in three children—almost 4 million.

The HBAI measure shows the same groups suffer from poverty as in the PSE Survey. The main explanation for poverty is no wage or low wage. No wage includes the unemployed and the elderly. The poor unemployed mainly consist of lone parents and the disabled. Low pay particularly affects those doing part-time work. Almost a third of all those in income poverty live in

households containing someone in paid work and in half of these cases, the work is part-time. Children are affected as members of workless families and families living on a low income.

Extent of poverty according to Income Support level

Using the Income Support (IS) level as the measure for poverty would significantly reduce the number of people classed as poor. In 2005, the IS level for a couple with two children was £178. This is £82 lower than the HBAI measure which means that the IS level is only 68% of the HBAI level. This would eliminate a large proportion of the population. For a lone parent

A breakdown of the people living in income poverty in Scotland

Household work status	Household type	Number living in poverty	Proportion of the group living in poverty
Workless households	Unemployed	90,000	75%
	Workless long-term sick or disabled	200,000	55%
	Workless lone parents	180,000	75%
Working, but low paid, households	Part-time work only	130,000	35%
	Some full-time work	150,000	5%
Pensioners	Not claiming Pension Credit	60,000	60%
	Claiming Pension Credit	140,000	15%
Total		950,000	20%

Table 2.4

Source: NPI estimates based on the Households Below Average Income dataset, DWP
(website: http://www.jrf.org.uk/knowledge/findings/socialpolicy/0585.asp#table2)

with two children the IS level is only £147, compared to £180 for the HBAI, which means that the IS level is only 82% of the HBAI level. Even this figure would prevent a high number of people from being classed as poor. Therefore we can conclude that the government approved levels of benefit for those not able to work long term are very low.

SOCIAL EXCLUSION

Social exclusion is complex to explain because it has many causes. It is the result of the big economic, industrial and social changes which have taken place over the last twenty to thirty years and the government policies that either were partly responsible for these changes or were a response to them. These changes caused or contributed to long-term or repeated unemployment, family instability, social isolation and the decline of neighbourhood and social networks.

Social exclusion occurs as a result of shortcomings and failures in the systems and structures of family, community and society. It occurs when individuals are separated from employment, social relations, and social systems. (See Figure 2.3.) However individuals, and the way in which they respond to events, also have a responsibility for their own social exclusion.

Children born into a lifestyle where adults place little or no value on education, where unemployment and short-term working is normal, where diets are poor and housing is of low quality, and where crime and substance abuse are commonplace will find it extremely difficult to escape into a better life cycle. They are most likely to remain in the cycle of poverty, stuck in the underclass in which they were brought up.

The PSE survey described social exclusion as exclusion from

- adequate income or resources
- the labour market
- services
- social relations

Exclusion from adequate income or resources

People are excluded from adequate income and resources for a variety of reasons. They may be unemployed or may have a large family and be working in a low paid job. They may be part of a lone parent family living on welfare benefits or a pensioner surviving on the state pension. Whatever the reason they do not have an income sufficient to gain access to all the things that the majority of people believed to be necessities in the PSE survey. There are one in four people, and one in three children, living in poverty.

Exclusion from the labour market

Unemployment affects all aspects of social exclusion. It means having an inadequate income and if it persists for long periods it will continue into old age.

Exclusion from services

Access to health, education and housing is a basic human right.

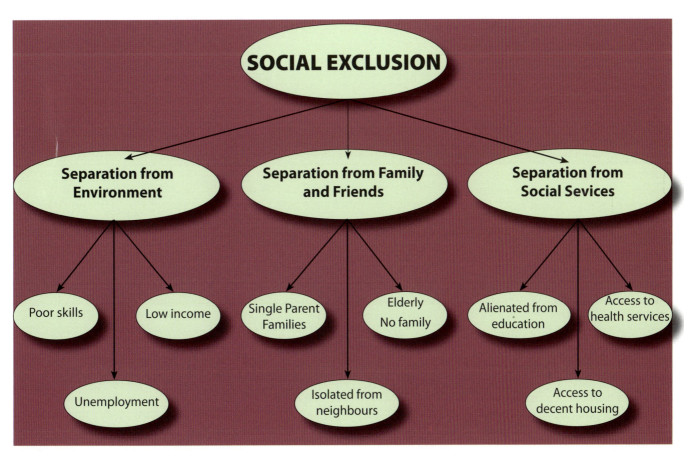

Figure 2.3

However, many are excluded. Over 5% of the population have been disconnected from water, gas, electricity or telephone and more than 10% say they cannot afford to use them as often as they need. The PSE survey found that 7% of the population are excluded from four or more essential services and nearly 25% are excluded from two or more because they are unaffordable.

Exclusion from social relations

10% of the population are excluded from five or more activities on the list of social activities such as celebrating a birthday or going to a wedding. 20% of the population say they are excluded from three or more of these activities. 12% of the population say they have no contact on a daily basis with a friend, neighbour or family member outside their home.

People who care for others—young, sick or disabled—say they lack the time to be able to participate in socially necessary activities. Disability is also an obstacle which leads to social exclusion and men who live alone are at high risk of social isolation.

The growth of social exclusion in the UK

Between 1979 and 2000 poverty increased dramatically in the UK. The reasons were political, economic and social. Politically, the policies of the Conservative governments between 1979 and 1997 made changes to the taxation and benefits systems in the UK which helped those on high incomes to retain more of their wealth and reduced the benefits paid to those in need of assistance.

At the same time the economic changes that were taking place created massive job losses in many well-paid manual jobs and created many low paid service industry jobs. The population was also ageing and more elderly people were living longer in poverty.

THE DEBATE

Society creates wealth and poverty

Some argue that the class a person is born into is what dominates their life chances. It is clear from the evidence that being born into poverty greatly increases a person's chances of living their life in poverty. An underclass exists where poverty is concentrated and has a major influence on keeping people trapped in a cycle of poverty.

The influence of poverty is passed on down the generations making it difficult for individuals to break out because of pressures from poor housing, limiting environment, poor educational experience, negative role models and peer group pressures.

Some would argue that society does not do enough to help people with their personal circumstances which can make them poor. Events like having children, suffering from long-term illness or disability, being unemployed and growing old can all have an impact. Each will reduce the opportunities available to earn an income and at the same time place additional burdens on expenditure. Although society spends a great deal on helping people in these situations some would argue that it is not enough.

These people would argue that taxes should be increased to allow benefits and other forms of help to be increased.

Individuals create wealth and poverty

Some people argue that the prime cause of poverty is an individual's behaviour. Individuals have choices, so the poor must choose to be poor. An underclass has detached itself from society and it is created by individuals who choose to live this way. Welfare dependency weakens people's will to work and therefore leads them into poverty.

Some divide society into the deserving poor and the undeserving poor. The deserving poor are those who have reduced circumstances through no fault of their own, such as children and the elderly. The undeserving poor are the unemployed who are fit but who do not take any job on offer, substance abusers who are unfit to work and other similar groups.

These people would argue that taxes should be reduced to encourage people to work by allowing them to keep more of their income, and reducing benefit expenditure by targeting benefits only on the deserving poor.

Social attitudes towards marriage and divorce changed significantly in the last thirty years of the twentieth century and so created a significant increase in the number of lone parent families in the UK. We will consider seven main reasons for poverty in the UK and review the political, economic and social impact these have. We will also study the impact that government policies, unemployment, low income employment, disability, age, gender and race have on poverty.

GOVERNMENT POLICY – TAXATION

When the welfare state was introduced in 1948, the government took on the responsibility of trying to reduce poverty. Progressive taxation is one way to redistribute wealth. Progressive taxation means the more a person earns the more they pay in tax. If income tax rates increase as a person earns more, then so does the amount they pay in tax. Therefore money is taken from the rich and redistributed to the poor through the welfare system.

When the Labour Party became the government in 1997, it did so on a policy of not increasing taxation to any extent. Consequently, with the tax burden falling on those with the lowest incomes in the UK, no radical changes could be made to the tax structure to help the poorest. Certain groups have been targeted with assistance such as families with children with Working Tax Credit and pensioners with Winter Fuel Allowance and Pension Credits. However, these measures have not been able to reduce the burden of taxation for the poorest.

Currently the burden of direct taxation is progressive with those in the top 20% earnings bracket paying 24% of their earnings in income tax and those in the bottom 20% paying only 12% of their incomes. However, when we look at indirect taxation those in the bottom 20% income bracket give 30% of their incomes in VAT and excise duties whereas those in the top 20% only pay 10% of their incomes in indi-

Progressive & Regressive TAXES

Progressive Tax—the more that is earned the higher the amount of tax paid. Income tax can be used as a progressive tax.

For example, on incomes up to £20,000 the tax rate is 10%; on the next £10,000 the tax rate is 20%; on the next £10,000 the tax rate is 50%; and on the rest the tax rate is 80%. Therefore a person earning £50,000 would be required to pay

10% of first £20,000	=	£2,000
20% of next £10,000	=	£2,000
50% of next £10,000	=	£5,000
80% of next £10,000	=	£8,000

} £17,000 in tax which is 34% of their income.

A person earning £100,000 would pay £57,000 in tax because the extra £50,000 would be taxed at 80% which is £40,000. This is 57% of their income. Therefore the more you earn the more you pay.

Regressive Tax—the more a person earns the smaller the proportion of their income they pay in tax. VAT is an example of a regressive tax.

If you buy a car and VAT is 20% then the tax you pay on a £10,000 car is £2,000.

If the income is £100,000 per year then the VAT of £2,000 is 2% of the income.
If the income is £20,000 per year then the VAT of £2,000 is 10% of the income.
If the income is £10,000 per year then the VAT of £2,000 is 20% of the income.
If the income is £5,000 per year then the VAT of £2,000 is 40% of the income.

Therefore the more you earn the smaller the proportion of your income you pay in tax.

With a progressive taxation system the amount paid in tax increases the more a person earns and so the burden of tax is on the rich. With a regressive tax the amount paid in tax decreases the more a person earns and so the burden of tax is on the poor.

The Burden of taxation in the UK

	Percentage of income taken in tax		
INCOME GROUP	DIRECT TAX	INDIRECT TAX	TOTAL TAX
Top 20%	24%	10%	34%
Next 20%	21%	15%	36%
Next 20%	18%	18%	36%
Next 20%	13%	20%	33%
Bottom 20%	12%	30%	42%

Table 2.5

Source: *The Burden of Taxation* – Ian Townsend, House of commons Library

rect taxes. This means that overall the bottom 20% of income earners pay 42% of their incomes in tax while those at the top end only pay 34%. (See Table 2.5.)

If the government chose it could reduce the level of VAT and replace it with an increase in income tax. This would restructure the tax burden from the poor to the rich and reduce the income gap. However, the government committed itself to no significant increase in direct taxation so it cannot alter the burden of tax to any great extent.

GOVERNMENT POLICY – THE BENEFIT SYSTEM

Benefit levels are a political decision. The Department of Work and Pensions, taking its lead from the Treasury, decides the level of benefits and these are approved by Parliament. Historically, increases in benefit levels are linked either to the annual increase in earnings, or to annual inflation.

For the past thirty years successive governments have used annual inflation as their benchmark for benefit increases. As earnings have increased faster than inflation over this period, the value of benefits has fallen behind earnings.

Recent government policy has been to increase marginally the amount spent overall on benefit payments while restructuring the groups at whom benefits are targeted. In the last ten years spending on social security has risen by 2% to 12% of GNP which is 30% of all government expenditure.

There has also been a shift in emphasis towards helping pensioners and families with children alongside measures to encourage people to move from benefits into work. As a result there has been a sharp decline in the number of unemployed claimants, and a smaller decline in the number of lone parent claimants. Unemployed households and some lone parent households are moving into low income jobs encouraged by working family benefits which boost income levels.

However, the number of sick and disabled claimants continues to grow. For a time it was government policy to reduce the statistics for unemployment by shifting claimants from benefits for unemployment to benefits for long-term disability.

The UK benefit system is very complex. It often confuses or puts off some groups, such as pensioners, from making claims for benefits to which they are entitled. Those who administer the system often make

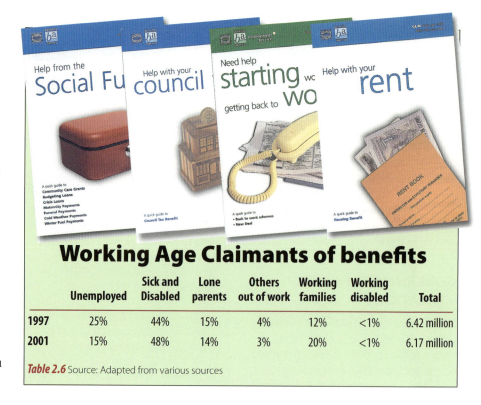

Working Age Claimants of benefits

	Unemployed	Sick and Disabled	Lone parents	Others out of work	Working families	Working disabled	Total
1997	25%	44%	15%	4%	12%	<1%	6.42 million
2001	15%	48%	14%	3%	20%	<1%	6.17 million

Table 2.6 Source: Adapted from various sources

mistakes. So people are frequently denied benefit or are overpaid and this costs the taxpayer millions of pounds each year.

According to the National Audit Office, the Department for Work and Pensions (DWP) lost £2.6 billion in 2005 due to errors. The introduction of new benefits and the constant flow of change has made the system difficult to understand for both staff and claimants. Each month the DWP sends out 600 million payments to about 30 million people.

Pensioners as a group are particularly vulnerable. According to Help the Aged, pensioners failed to claim £2.5 billion in benefits to which they were entitled. There are twenty three benefits available to older people but the system is muddled. Barely 50% of pensioners entitled to Pension Credit claim it and even fewer claim Council Tax Benefit.

Many do not know what they are entitled to because it is not adequately brought to their attention. Even if they do know, the system is so complex that negotiating their way around it is a struggle. Finally, most benefits are means-tested. Many older people do not wish to disclose such personal information,

and some would rather go without benefits than endure intrusive questioning.

INTERNATIONAL COMPARISON OF BENEFITS

The UK is more than halfway down the list of EU countries for benefit spending. It is ahead of some of the poorer European countries such as Portugal and Greece, but lags behind the richer ones such as Germany and Luxembourg. It also does less than other European countries to reduce inequality through the tax and benefit systems.

Figure 2.4 shows that the UK tax and benefit systems do less than the systems of our European neighbours to reduce the proportion of households whose incomes are less than half the average income. For example, the UK is similar to Belgium, Sweden and Denmark in having around 40% of its households with incomes of less than half the average income. However, after the effect of tax and benefits the UK still has 25% of its households with incomes less than half the average income, while the proportion in Belgium, Sweden and Denmark has fallen to under 10%.

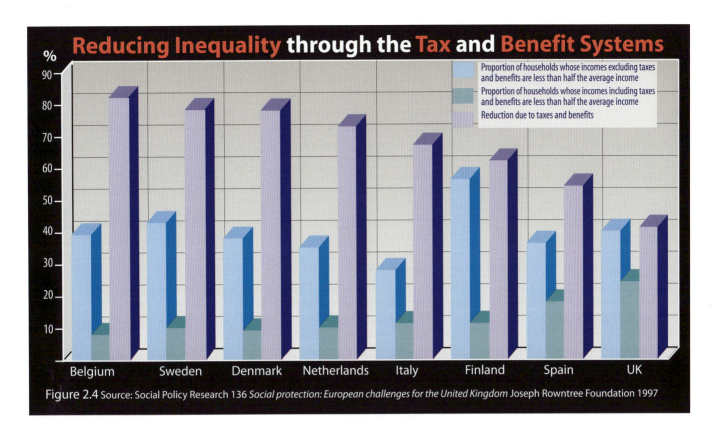

Reducing Inequality through the Tax and Benefit Systems

Legend:
- Proportion of households whose incomes excluding taxes and benefits are less than half the average income
- Proportion of households whose incomes including taxes and benefits are less than half the average income
- Reduction due to taxes and benefits

Countries: Belgium, Sweden, Denmark, Netherlands, Italy, Finland, Spain, UK

Figure 2.4 Source: Social Policy Research 136 *Social protection: European challenges for the United Kingdom* Joseph Rowntree Foundation 1997

EMPLOYMENT AND UNEMPLOYMENT LEVELS

The level of unemployment fell between 1997 and 2001. Since then it has fluctuated slightly but has remained fairly stable around the 5% level. In 2006, this represented 1.53 million people who were unemployed and seeking work. UK levels of unemployment are significantly better than those of some of the other large economic partners in the EU. In 2006, both France with 9.2% and Germany at 9.5% had nearly double the UK rate.

In 2006, the employment rate was 74.5% of those of working age. There were 28.8 million people working in the UK.

UK Unemployment 1997 – 2006 (%)

Year	%
1997	6.8
2001	5.0
2006	5.0

Table 2.7 Source: ONS

Structure of the UK Economy

Sector	Alternative Name	Industries included in sector	Percentage of workers employed
Primary	Primary Industries	Farming Forestry Fishing Mining and quarrying	2%
Secondary	Manufacturing Industries	Processing raw materials Manufacturing Construction	22%
Tertiary	Service Industries	Retail Tourism Education Health Banking	76%

Table 2.8

Structural and technological change – unemployment and low pay

As Table 2.8 shows, the UK economy is divided into three sectors—primary, secondary and tertiary. The economy is always changing. Jobs are created and jobs disappear in different sectors of the economy as a result of changes in demand and changes in technology.

The UK has changed from being a society where most people were involved in primary industries, through a period when manufacturing industries were dominant, to the present day in which 76% of the working population are involved in service industries. Jobs in the service industries increased by 45%, from 14.8 million in 1978 to 21.5 million in 2005, while those in manufacturing fell by 54% from 6.9 million to 3.2 million over the same period.

These changes have been brought on by technological developments. As agriculture, forestry and fishing became increasingly mechanised, work in the primary sector of the economy was reduced to its current level of 2% of the total workforce. Workers were then needed in manufacturing. However, as heavy engineering gave way to light engineering and eventually to electronics and robotics, jobs disappeared in this sector and many that remained were affected by deskilling. Today the service sector provides over three-quarters of the employment in the UK economy.

Currently, financial and business services account for 20% of the jobs in the UK, whereas twenty years ago it was only 10%. Over the same period the number of jobs held by men in manufacturing has fallen from one in three to one in five.

Figure 2.5 shows that the process is on-going with jobs still being lost in primary and secondary industry in Scotland between 1995 and 2000, and continuing to increase in the service sector.

Technological and structural change creates unemployment. Where new jobs are introduced different skills are required which may leave a pool of unemployed people who do not have these skills. Change creates some new jobs which are highly paid because a high degree of skill is necessary but many more that are low paid because of the low skill level required.

Wage inequality between highly skilled workers and unskilled workers has increased significantly in the last twenty five years. The relative value of the wages of skilled workers increased on average 1.7% more than the wages of unskilled workers each year between 1980 and 2005. Over that period the gap in wages between skilled and unskilled workers grew by 35% in favour of the skilled workers.

GOVERNMENT POLICY AND UNEMPLOYMENT

Through its Budget the government has a major influence on the economy. In 2005, it raised £508.1 billion in taxes and spent over £548.3 billion. How it chooses to raise this amount and how it decides to spend it will have an enormous impact on employment in the UK.

If the Chancellor decides to spend more than is raised in taxation then the government will increase the level of economic activity in the country. By running a series of deficits and making up the difference by borrowing, the government increases the amount of money in circulation. This means that people will have more to spend and will buy more goods and services. This in turn means that more goods will be made and manufacturing and service providers will employ more people to provide for the increased demand. House prices will rise and wealth will increase.

Nevertheless, this cannot go on for ever as both inflation and imports from foreign suppliers will increase. This will harm the UK Balance of Trade which in turn will reduce the value of the pound, causing the prices of imports to rise. Increased prices will reduce demand and increase unemployment.

If the Chancellor raises more in taxation than the government spends then money will be taken out of the economy. People will buy less and manufacturers and service providers will have to cut back. Unemployment will rise. In particular, unemployment among the low skilled workers will increase quickly as they are more easily replaced when things improve.

The government has a major impact on regional unemployment by deciding the areas in which to spend money. It can create unemployment in one region if it reduces the amount it spends in that area and increase employment opportunities in another area if it increases spending. For example, it closed a naval dockyard in South Fife thus creating unemployment, moving the work capacity to Portsmouth where employment was increased.

Government spending has an impact on workers with different levels of skill. If it reduces the number of cleaners in the NHS and increases the number of managers, then it will increase levels of unemployment among manual workers

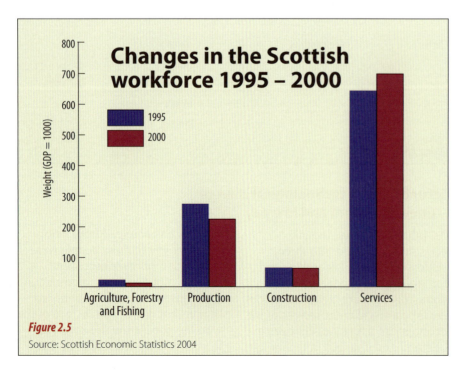

Changes in the Scottish workforce 1995 – 2000

- 1995
- 2000

Weight (GDP = 1000)

Agriculture, Forestry and Fishing   Production   Construction   Services

Figure 2.5
Source: Scottish Economic Statistics 2004

and reduce unemployment for more highly paid skilled workers.

Specific government policy towards the unemployed will have a significant impact on unemployment levels. Over several years successive governments have encouraged older and long-term unemployed people to move to claiming disability benefits. This has significantly increased the number of people classed as disabled but at the same time has reduced the official unemployment rate. Governments have also made many changes to the way unemployment is calculated, most of which have statistically reduced unemployment levels.

Since 1997, successive Labour governments have created a benefit system that makes it increasingly difficult for groups of people to remain on benefits, while providing incentives for them to move into work. This has reduced the level of unemployment in the UK.

Education and unemployment

Educational attainment differs by social class. Figure 2.6 shows that more than twice as many children of higher professional parents gained five or more GCSE grades compared to children whose parents were in lower social class groups. Table 2.9 shows the impact that education has on levels of employment. Those with degree or equivalent qualifications had nearly double the employment rates of those with no qualifications. The statistics were more marked for women than for men.

As structural and technological changes take place in the economy there is less and less demand for those with few or no skills or little education. Many low skill jobs have been exported to developing countries where wage rates are much lower than in the UK.

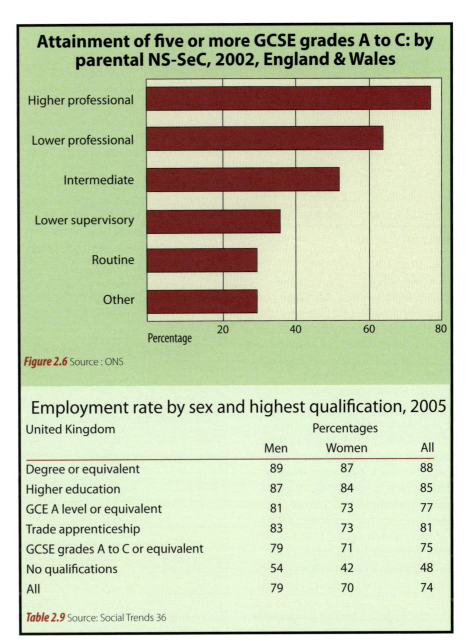

Figure 2.6 Source : ONS

Employment rate by sex and highest qualification, 2005

United Kingdom		Percentages	
	Men	Women	All
Degree or equivalent	89	87	88
Higher education	87	84	85
GCE A level or equivalent	81	73	77
Trade apprenticeship	83	73	81
GCSE grades A to C or equivalent	79	71	75
No qualifications	54	42	48
All	79	70	74

Table 2.9 Source: Social Trends 36

Age and Unemployment

As people get older it becomes more difficult to find employment. In 2004, the employment rate for those aged 50 – 54 was 79%. It fell sharply to 67.7% for those aged 55 – 59 and to 41% for those 60 – 64. Only 5.9% of those over 65 were employed.

Although Table 2.10 appears to suggest that the unemployment rate for those over 50 is the lowest of all age groups, it is because unemployment is being hidden. In the 50 to 65 age group, 52% of those who are economically inactive are described as long-term sick and disabled while a further 30% are classed as retired. Many have been pushed into these categories because of the limited opportunities available

Unemployment Rate by Age and Gender (%): January 2006

	All	Male	Female
All 16+	5.0	5.3	4.7
16–17	24.9	28.1	21.8
18–24	11.5	12.6	10.1
24–49	3.7	3.8	3.7
50+	2.9	3.4	2.3

Table 2.10 Source: ONS

to them to find employment. Older workers in the UK are 25% more likely than younger workers to be either unemployed or economically inactive.

Nearly 600,000 people of working age describe themselves as retired.

Unemployed over 12 months by Age and Gender (%): January 2006			
	All	Male	Female
All 16+	21.0	25.8	15.2
16–17	6.6	--	--
18–24	15.2	18.4	10.7
25–49	23.9	29.2	17.5
50+	37.5	42.9	27.5

Table 2.11 Source: ONS

Of these, 400,000 are men and 200,000 are women. Although some may have made a positive decision to retire, the majority have not done so voluntarily. Medical grounds and redundancy are the most common reasons for early retirement.

There are many more older workers out of work for twelve months or more. Table 2.11 shows that those over the age of 50 find great difficulty in finding re-employment. This is largely due to age discrimination by employers. In a recent study, researchers submitted CVs for two women aged 21 and 39 who had "graduated simultaneously with degrees in economics or law". The 39-year-old graduate received interview invitations at only 38% of the rate enjoyed by the 21-year-old.

A second study created two waiters aged 27 and 47 and submitted CVs across England. Despite having a CV that showed he was fit and had twenty years more experience, the middle-aged waiter received interview invitations at only 60% of the rate enjoyed by the 27-year-old. In London he got only 25% of interview invitations.

Age, then, has a significant impact on unemployment mainly due to age discrimination by employers, but it is largely hidden because the statistics for older workers who are made redundant are converted into figures for economic inactivity such as retirement and long-term illness and disability. Those older workers who do try to obtain work find the duration of their unemployment very much lengthened.

INCOME INEQUALITIES IN THE UK

There are big differences in income between people who work at different jobs and in different sectors of the UK economy. Table 2.12 shows that the top 10% earn at least four times as much as the bottom 10%. Highest average earnings were in the financial sectors such as banks and insurance, in computer-related industries and in radio and television, whereas hotels and restaurants, farming, retail and bar work paid the least. (See Table 2.13.)

Among the highest paid occupations are directors and chief executives of major organisations who earned on average £2,301 per week in 2003, followed by medical practitioners on £1,186 and financial managers and chartered secretaries (£1,124). Solicitors and lawyers, judges and coroners earned £925 per week and marketing and sales managers on £888 complete the top five groups of workers in the UK.

The lowest paid earned only one-tenth of the income of directors and chief executives. Retail cashiers and check-out operators earned on average £207 per week. (See Table 2.14.)

Full-time gross weekly earnings including overtime pay (April 2003)			
	Men	Women	All
10% earned less than	£243.8	£202.0	£222.7
50% earned less than	£431.9	£338.6	£394.3
10% earned more than	£854.9	£634.2	£770.0

Table 2.12 Source: New earnings Survey 2003

Highest and Lowest paid industry groups 2003
Average gross earnings per week (£)

Highest paid

1	Financial	798.3
2	Computer related activities	768.0
3	Software consultancy and supply	754.1
4	Radio and television activities	691.3
5	Manufacture of pharmaceuticals medicinal chemicals and botanical products	673.5

Lowest paid

1	Hotels	287.8
2	Restaurants	305.3
3	Mixed farming	306.7
4	Retail sale of food, beverages and tobacco in specialised stores	309.8

Table 2.13
Source: New Earnings Survey 2003

Low Income Employment

Low income employment is a major cause of poverty. Through lack of education and skill many people are forced to take low paid jobs. Despite the introduction of the National Minimum Wage (NMW), the Annual Survey of Hours and Earnings estimated that in 2005 there were 327,000 jobs which paid below the NMW. This amounted to 1.3% of all jobs in the labour market.

77,000 of these low paid jobs were held by those aged 16 to 21 while 250,000 jobs were held by people aged 22 and over. People in part-time work were two and half times more likely than people in full-time work to be paid less than the minimum wage. More women than men were in this group as more had part-time jobs.

Even those who are paid the National Minimum Wage face poverty. In 2003–04, the HBAI measure of poverty for a family of two adults and two children was an income of £260 per week. The NMW was £4.85 per hour in 2003–04 giving someone a gross income of £194 for forty hours of work which is more than £60 lower than the HBAI measure for poverty. This is before tax and other deductions and before Family Tax Credit is applied. However, there are still many households who earn poverty wages every week.

Table 2.14 shows that the lowest paid workers in the UK are check-out operators. Most low paid jobs are in retail, bar, restaurant and hotel work as well as services such as hairdressing and laundry work.

Just over half of working age adults who are in poverty live in households where at least one person is working. That is 2.6 million people. For most, being a low paid worker is not temporary. People who work in low paid jobs tend to remain in this type of work. These jobs tend not to be a step on the ladder to higher paid employment. Most low paid jobs have no prospects for promotion nor are they useful as

Lowest paid jobs in UK	
Average Gross Weekly Pay 2003 (£)	
1 Retail cashiers and check-out operators	207.6
2 Launderers, dry cleaners, pressers	217.6
3 Bar staff	217.9
4 Waiters, waitresses	218.2
5 Kitchen and catering assistants	228.4
6 Hotel porters	229.9
7 Hairdressers, barbers	231.8
8 Animal care occupations	232.3
9 Sewing machinists	239.8
10 Shelf fillers	241.5

Table 2.14 Source: New Earnings Survey 2003

experience when applying for better paid posts.

Low paid jobs are often transient. Many are trapped in the 'low pay, no pay' cycle in which periods of low pay are interspersed with periods of unemployment. In 2004, only 45% of those who were made redundant had found work within three months. Therefore many people find themselves facing long periods of unemployment interspersed with short periods of low paid work.

Successive periods of unemployment make it more difficult for a person to get a new job and the longer the period of unemployment the greater the difficulty. Those who are unemployed find they can only aspire to low paid work which often ends after a few months and continues to prevent them finding a route out of poverty.

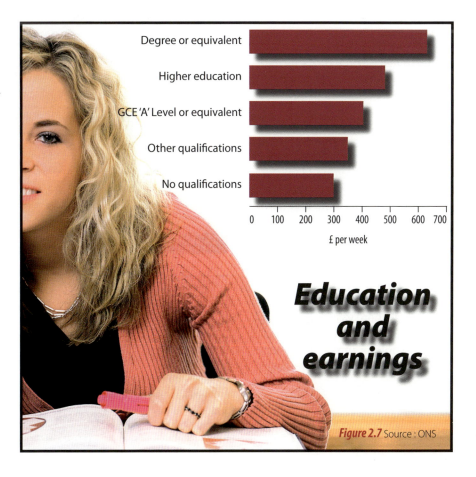

Figure 2.7 Source : ONS

Education and Earnings

There is a clear relationship between higher qualifications and higher earnings. (See Figure 2.7.) In the UK, the average gross weekly income of full-time employees in the UK with a degree was £632 in spring 2003. This was more than double the weekly income of £298 for those with no qualifications.

Social class affects education. More than 50% of those studying medicine and dentistry, and nearly half of those studying law and engineering are from the highest two groups. These subjects prepare students to get the highest paid jobs.

Education influences the level of earnings and it also helps to perpetuate class divisions across the generations. Children from higher social classes are disproportionately well represented at the higher levels of education compared with children from lower social class groups so will go on to better paid, higher class occupations.

Part-time Work and poverty

Just over one-quarter of the UK workforce worked part-time in 2006. 20% of the workforce were women working part-time, while 6% were men. Three times as many women as men were part-time workers.

Those working part-time earn considerably less than those working full-time. In 2003, 50% of those working part-time earned less than £124 a week before deductions with the bottom 10% earning less than £43 per week.

Whether a person is able to work full-time or part-time has a major impact on their relative poverty. Even those who were in the top 10% of part-time workers earning around £300 per week gross would be living not far above the poverty line unless they had an alternative source of income.

Degree course undergraduates by class for selected subjects (%)

NS-SeC	Medicine & Dentistry	Engineering	Law	Business	Total (all subjects)
1 Higher managerial and professional occupations	34.1	20.6	20.0	14.9	17.0
2 Lower managerial and professional occupations	25.3	23.9	27.0	25.4	24.5
3 Intermediate occupations	9.5	10.8	12.0	12.0	12.1
4 Small employers and own account workers	4.2	6.0	5.9	7.3	6.0
5 Lower supervisory and technical occupations	2.2	6.3	3.8	4.4	4.0
6 Semi-routine occupations	6.0	11.8	9.9	11.5	10.9
7 Routine occupations	2.0	4.3	4.7	5.8	4.7
8 Unknown	16.6	16.3	16.0	18.7	20.7

Table 2.15 Source: ONS

Employment in the UK 2006

		(000)	%
All	full-time	21,501	74
	part-time	7,305	26
	total	28,806	100
Male	full-time	13,891	48
	part-time	1,665	6
Female	full-time	7,610	26
	part-time	5,640	20
	total	28,806	100

Table 2.16 Source: Labour Force Survey

Part-time gross weekly earnings including overtime pay
(April 2003)

	Men	Women	All
10% earned less than	£39.0	£44.6	£43.2
50% earned less than	£113.6	£126.0	£124.0
10% earned more than	£307.1	£276.7	£280.8

Table 2.17 Source: New earnings Survey 2003

CHILDREN

There are three times as many children living in poverty as there were twenty five years ago. HBAI statistics show that 3.5 million children are living in income poverty which is 29% of children in the UK. Children are more likely to face poverty because of the cost to a household of bringing up a family. Particular groups of children are more likely to live in poverty.

The larger the family the more likely they are to suffer from poverty. In 2002 a third of all children lived in families with three or more children. (See Table 2.18.) Table 2.19 shows that as family size increases children are more likely to live in low income households. 49% of children in families with four or more children live in households which have the bottom 20% of household income and four out of five children in these large families live in households with the bottom 40% of income. As it costs more to bring up more children, larger families are obviously far more likely to live in poverty.

Another group of children facing poverty are those who live in workless households. HBAI statistics show that four out of five children (79%) in households where no adult is working were living in income poverty. However, having a working parent or working parents does not guarantee a route out of poverty for children. 32% of children in households with at least one adult working and 11% of children in households with both adults in work were also living in poverty.

Family structure is also a factor. Over half (52%) of children in lone parent households lived in income poverty compared with 21% of children in couple households.

Children living in ethnic minority households were more likely than children in white households to live in poverty, although different ethnic groups face different rates of child poverty. 26% of white children live in income poverty, compared

Percentage of lone parent and couple families by size of family 2001/02

Number of dependent children	Children in lone parent families	Children in couple families	Total of all children in families	Number in millions
One	50%	37%	22%	2.9
Two	33%	44%	44%	5.7
Three or more	17%	19%	33%	4.3
Total	3.1 million	9.6 million	12.8 million	

Table 2.18

Percentage of children in bottom quintiles (fifths) by household income and family size 2001/02

Number of dependent children	Bottom 20% of household income	Bottom 40% of household income
One	19	41
Two	19	44
Three	32	61
Four or more	49	80

Table 2.19

Source: Hilary Land *Women, child poverty and childcare* Bristol University 2004

with 75% of Pakistani/Bangladeshi children, 53% of black non-Caribbean children, 39% of black Caribbean children and 22% of Indian children.

The age of both adults and children in a household affects child poverty rates. In families where the youngest child is under 5 years old, 32% of children live in poverty, compared with 29% for the youngest child being aged 5 to 10 years, 24% for the 11 to 15 group and 20% for youngest being 16 to 18. With younger children, mothers are less likely to get suitable employment. For mothers aged under 25 years, 53% of their children were in poverty, compared to 33% for mothers in the 30 to 34 age group.

If a member of the household has a disability it increases poverty rates. 39% of children in households with a disabled adult were in poverty, compared with 26% where there was no disabled adult. In households with at least one disabled child 31% of children live in poverty, compared with 28% of children in households with no disabled children.

Child poverty varies across different geographical areas of the UK. Child poverty in Wales was slightly higher at 30% compared with 29% for England and 27% in Scotland. At a regional level the differences are even greater. London had the highest child poverty rate in Britain with 38% for Greater

London, rising to 54% in Inner London.

Internationally, the UK has a comparatively high child poverty rate. Figures from the European Community Household Panel Survey show that in 2001 the UK ranked eleventh out of the fifteen European Union nations on child poverty rates.

A Comparison of Housing Tenure (%)

	Owned outright	Owned with mortgage	Rented from social sector	Rented privately	All tenures
Retired	65	6	25	4	100
All groups	30	39	20	11	100

Table 2.20 Source: Social Trends 36

The availability of good quality childcare is central to breaking the cycle of child poverty.

The Cycle of Child Poverty

Poverty is very localised. Although one child in four lives in poverty, there are some wards where 90% of children are poor. Poverty is about the struggle of poor families to give their children the chance to grow and thrive. Growing up in poverty can affect every area of a child's development—social, educational and personal.

Poor children have poor diets and health, live in sub-standard housing, have nowhere safe to play and are more likely to die in an accident. They are smaller at birth and shorter in height. They do less well at school and have poor school attendance.

In the long term they grow up to be adults who are more likely to suffer ill health, be unemployed or homeless. They are more likely to become involved in offending, drug and alcohol abuse and abusive relationships. Most remain in the same income bracket as their parents, so the cycle perpetuates itself.

The availability of good quality childcare is central to breaking the cycle. Childcare enables parents to work or train for jobs, and it gives children a head start in life. Care and education in the early years improves children's educational achievement and health. There are 600,000 children under three living in poverty and only 43,000 free or subsidised childcare places. Almost all childcare services are private sector arrangements for those whose parents can pay.

ELDERLY PEOPLE AND POVERTY

The number of elderly people as a proportion of the total population is growing. In 1971 there were 7.4 million people aged 65 and over and by 2004 this had increased to 9.6 million. By 2014 projections suggest that the number of people over 65 will exceed the number under 16 for the first time.

The dependency ratio is the balance between the number of people of working age and those over state pension age. Today the dependency ratio is 27% which means there are around three workers for each pensioner. By 2050, it will be 47%, or one pensioner for each worker. As the dependency ratio increases, will those in work be able to support an ever-ageing population with its demands on pensions and its need for increased health care? Will pensioner poverty grow to the point where increasing numbers of elderly people die as a result?

Some pensioner households are very well off. Those who have had a good job, worked all their lives, avoided family break ups and have enjoyed good health will be very comfortably off. They are at the point in their life cycle where they are the wealthiest they will ever be. They own their own home (see Table 2.20), which is mortgage free, and they will have savings. They have pension entitlement from the state, any private pension they have invested in and perhaps an occupational pension. As they get older they will use up some or all of their wealth depending on their health, which may necessitate care provision.

However, there are a significant number of pensioner households who will face poverty. Those whose working lives have been affected by unemployment or low income employment, family separation and divorce, or disability may well face poverty in their retirement.

In Scotland, as in the rest of the UK, pensioner poverty has been falling from an average of 28% of all pensioners in the mid-1990s to 20% in recent years. According to the official figures pensioners are now no more likely to be living in income poverty than non-pensioners. However, as Table 2.21 shows, apart from lone parents, a higher proportion of pensioners suffer from low incomes than all other groups in society.

Problems of being old

Poverty and social exclusion are increasingly serious and complex problems for the elderly. Poverty may exist in retirement as a continuation of poverty throughout a person's working life because they lack pensions, savings or home ownership as the result of facing life on a low income. This is intensified by other problems which can draw other, previously well-off, pensioners into poverty.

Ill health can increase due to advancing years but also due to poor diet and sub-standard housing conditions. Elderly people often live in older housing, which may be deteriorating through inattention or lack of income. Health can also suffer because of the conditions they worked in during their working lives or activities such as smoking or excessive alcohol use in their younger years. The largest single cause of ill health in older people is the effects of smoking throughout their lives.

Over one-third of people over 75 are disabled, the main cause of this being arthritis. Dementia is believed to disable about 5% of the elderly population. Both of these conditions can place a heavy strain on the finances of the elderly. Other problems may include isolation

Persistent low income
by family type, 2000–2003

Pensioner couple	17
Single pensioner	21
Couple with children	10
Couple without children	4
Single with children	23
Single without children	7
All individuals	11

Table 2.21
Source: Department for Work and Pensions from the British Household Panel Survey, Institute for Social and Economic Research

as friends and family die or move away. The death of a partner is a major source of bereavement.

Finally, the stress of caring for an elderly person who is physically or mentally disabled is highly intensified if the carer is also elderly.

Poverty and social exclusion, then, can intensify for elderly people as they get older. The biggest worries for the elderly are the lack of income to deal with the cost of living and coping with their increasing problems.

Recent research has found that 17% of pensioners have to survive on less than £5,000 a year, while 27% are struggling on between £5,000 and £10,000. Only 4% of pensioners have an income of more than £25,000 a year. 20% of pensioners said that their income was insufficient to meet their needs. 60% said they reduced their spending to make ends meet with 25% cutting back on buying clothes, 18% spending less on heating, 12% spending less on food and 6% reducing spending on visits to the doctor and buying medicine. Over half the pensioners said their pension would have to be increased significantly for them to enjoy a comfortable lifestyle.

One of the biggest problems facing the elderly is fuel poverty. According to Age Concern Scotland over 2,000 elderly people a year

are dying unnecessarily in Scotland because of fuel poverty. Around the UK, approximately 21,800 over-65s died due to cold weather in 2003. However, Age Concern Scotland claims that proportionately more older people die as a result of cold weather in Scotland than elsewhere in the UK.

Older people—especially the very old—suffer disproportionately from rising fuel costs because they tend to stay indoors more than other people and are most likely to feel the cold. The government's Fuel Poverty Advisory Group revealed that the number of households facing fuel poverty throughout the UK had almost doubled to 2.2 million between 2003 and 2006. Fuel poverty means having to spend more than 10% of disposable income on energy.

Pensioners may own their houses but their income is often too low to allow them to make repairs or improvements. According to Age Concern Scotland, "8,000 homes occupied by older people have been shown to be unfit for human occupation".

Increases in council tax are not tied to inflation or related to increases in pensions. Pensioners are particularly affected as they have difficulty increasing their income. According to Help the Aged, households in the average band D council tax band now face an average annual bill of £2,250 for council tax, water, gas and electricity alone. In other words, these basic living requirements eat up more than half the full basic state pension.

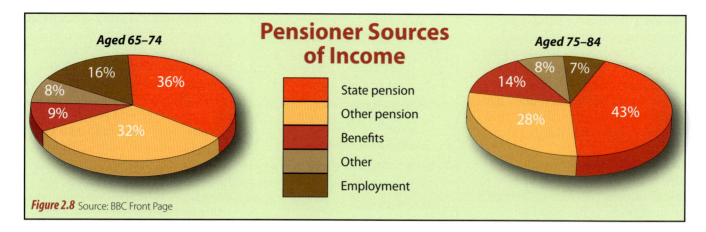

Pensioner Sources of Income

Aged 65–74

- 36% State pension
- 32% Other pension
- 9% Benefits
- 8% Other
- 16% Employment

Aged 75–84

- 43% State pension
- 28% Other pension
- 14% Benefits
- 8% Other
- 7% Employment

Legend:
- State pension
- Other pension
- Benefits
- Other
- Employment

Figure 2.8 Source: BBC Front Page

Most retired people depend on the state pension for their source of income. Figure 2.8 shows that elderly people depend on the state for their income more than on occupational or private pensions. However, the state pension is falling behind average earnings, so increasingly pensioners are in danger of falling into relative poverty.

In 1980 the government removed the link between state pensions and earnings. This meant that pensions would no longer be uprated in line with the average increase in earnings in the UK. As a result, the value of the basic state pension compared to average earnings has fallen. As Figure 2.9 shows the basic state pension was worth 21% of average earnings in 1980 but had fallen to 13% by 2005. As many pensioners depend on the state pension for most or all of their income, this means that increasing numbers of pensioners face poverty. (See page 61.)

Some pensioners were able to overcome the falling value of the state pension by being involved in a company pension scheme. However, many employers have closed their final salary pension schemes and replaced them with money purchase schemes in order to cut their financial contributions. New employees and many existing employees no longer have the prospect of a guaranteed final pension. Therefore in the future many more people will face retirement unsure of what their income will be or indeed if they will have any income at all from their occupational pension.

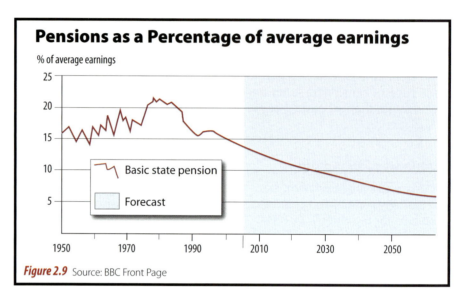

Pensions as a Percentage of average earnings

% of average earnings

- Basic state pension
- Forecast

Figure 2.9 Source: BBC Front Page

FINAL SALARY PENSION SCHEMES

In a final salary pension scheme both the employer and the employee contribute to a fund that guarantees a pension which is related to the level of the salary the person was earning just prior to retiral. If a person has made sufficient contributions to be entitled to a 50% pension based on a final years earnings of £40,000 then their pension will be £20,000 per year.

These final salary schemes are very expensive to run for the employer. By guaranteeing a level of pension based on final salary and length of service, companies depend on the contributions from existing employees and high levels of return from stock market investments to pay the pensions of those who have retired. If these sources of income decrease for any reason then the company has to pay the shortfall.

In the 1990s, the stock market downturn reduced the value of many funds. At the same time there was an increasing number of people retiring and living for a long time to claim their pension. Companies found they faced a huge shortfall in their schemes and many abandoned them.

MONEY PURCHASE SCHEMES

Many of the biggest employers now offer money purchase schemes. The employee has to take all the risk and the pension received is dependent on the performance of the investment in the stock market. If the stock market is rising the return is good, but in the early 2000s the markets collapsed and employees faced reduced pensions. With these schemes the retirement income a worker can expect to receive is uncertain.

Elderly women & poverty

Many elderly women are forced to live in greater poverty in old age than men because they have not acquired the same pension rights as men during their working years. There are nearly twice as many women pensioners as men but less than half receive the basic state pension and less than one-third of retired women qualify for the full basic state pension. (See Figure 2.10.) In 2003 the average basic state pension for a man was £73.45 per week. For a woman it was only £51.24. Over 70% of elderly, single women do not have a private pension and only half of female pensioners receive the full basic state pension.

As Table 3.19 on page 40 shows, women lose out in both occupational and personal pensions compared to men. Far more women than men work part-time which means they are at a particular disadvantage in terms of access to pensions. A government study found that, throughout his working life, a man saves three times as a much for a pension as a woman does.

Women lose out for choosing to take care of the children instead of working outside the home. As carers and lone parents, women tend to lose out on both continuous contributions for their state pension, and on the promotion that can provide for a reasonable level of income in retirement. They are forced into the complexities and indignities of means testing and consequently, through ignorance, pride or confusion, often do not get the level of income to which they are entitled.

Pensioners are likely to have difficulty dealing with new or complicated financial arrangements.

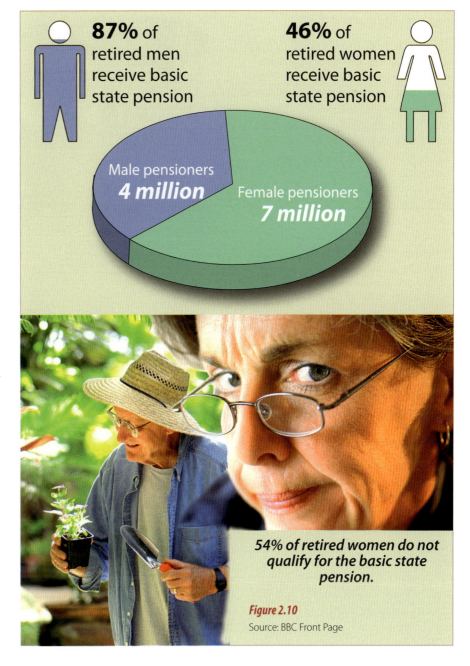

87% of retired men receive basic state pension

46% of retired women receive basic state pension

Male pensioners **4 million**

Female pensioners **7 million**

54% of retired women do not qualify for the basic state pension.

Figure 2.10
Source: BBC Front Page

Those who worked in lower paid jobs are the ones most likely to rely on means-tested benefits. These people often have a lower level of education which makes filling in the complicated forms even more of a challenge.

Not everyone claims their benefits. About a third of pensioners do not claim up to the Minimum Income Guarantee, leaving £1.9 billion of benefits left unclaimed by older people each year. Some pensioners do not know they can claim, some have difficulty completing the forms and some object to the intrusion and refuse to apply.

Finally, women live longer than men so their poverty is deeper and longer.

DISABLED AND POOR

There are 800,000 disabled people of working age who are 'economically inactive but want work'. The official figure for 'unemployed' disabled people is 200,000. The number of disabled adults who do not have work but want it is four times greater than the number included in the official figures.

In Scotland, 80% of long-term working age claimants of out-of-work benefits are sick or disabled, a further 15% are lone parents and only 2% are unemployed.

The majority of disabled people of working age wish to work.

In the UK, 30% of working age disabled adults live in income poverty, which is 3% more than ten years ago. Proportionately, this is higher than the rates for either pensioners or children. 29% of households with disabled people are poor, compared with 17% of households without disabled people. However, these statistics underestimate the true extent of poverty

among disabled people because they are based solely on income, including disability benefits, and do not take into account the additional costs disabled people may incur because of their disabilities.

Additional costs vary according to the type and degree of the disability. Additional costs may include food, clothing, household maintenance, fuel and power, household goods and services, transport, communications, recreation/culture, education, health, personal care, insurance and special occasions.

However, the biggest single cost is for personal assistance. 'Personal assistance' includes interpreters for deaf people, trainers for visually impaired people, and care services. For all groups of disabled people, the greatest need is for human assistance, rather than for adaptations and equipment.

REGIONS AND POVERTY

Poverty levels vary across the UK. Poverty appears to be greater in the north than in the south. In the south house prices and incomes are higher, health is better and unemployment rates are lower. Nevertheless, many argue that there is no north-south divide but that every area has pockets of wealth and poverty existing side by side.

Inequalities exist between regions and within regions of the UK. In Scotland, 1.1 million people (22%) live in low income households. There has been little change in the overall proportion of low income households over the past ten years. However, the proportion of pensioners and children living in low income households is falling while the proportion for working age adults without dependent children is increasing.

The pattern of poverty in Scotland mirrors that of the UK as a whole. Children (27%) remain much more likely to be living in low income households than adults (21%). This is mainly because around half of lone parent families are on low incomes. The poorest 10% of the population have 2% of Scotland's

The working age population 2003 (%)

	IN EMPLOYMENT			ECONOMICALLY INACTIVE	UNEMPLOYED
	Full-time	Part-time	Self-employed		
UK	49.7	15.9	8.6	21.4	4.9
Scotland	50.4	16.6	7.0	21.4	5.5

Table 2.22 Source: Regional Trends 38

total income, while the richest 10% have 27%. The overall distribution of income has changed little in ten years.

In Scotland there is a higher proportion of the working age population working both full-time and part-time but fewer people are self-employed. The unemployment rate is also higher than the UK average. For those working part-time, fewer people do so through choice. 21% of males and 9% of females who are in part-time work in Scotland want full-time employment compared to only 16% and 6% respectively for the whole of the UK.

The structure of the Scottish economy means that there are fewer jobs in high earning occupations and more in the lower supervisory and routine sectors. There are also more

people who have never worked or who are long-term unemployed. (See Table 2.26.)

Unemployment is higher in Scotland across all age groups and for all levels of education. (See Table 2.23.) This is despite the fact that Scottish school pupils gain signifi-

Unemployment by highest level of education 2003 (%)

	UK	Scotland
Higher education (below degree)	2.2	2.6
A level / H grade	3.8	4.7
GCSE / Standard Grade	5.5	8.2
No qualification	8.9	9.4

Table 2.23 Source: Regional Trends 38

Average weekly earnings
2002 (£)

	UK	Scotland
All	462.6	427.0
Male	511.3	473.7
Female	382.1	360.1

Table 2.24 Source: Regional Trends 38

Pupils achieving GCSE (A-C), SQA Standard Grade or equivalent (%)

		English	Maths	Science	French	Geography	History
All	UK	56.8	49.2	49.3	27.5	21.1	20.4
	Scotland	71.1	51.0	60.6	38.8	24.1	22.4
Male	UK	49.0	48.1	47.6	21.9	22.1	18.9
	Scotland	64.4	49.9	58.3	31.4	26.7	19.5
Female	UK	65.0	50.3	51.0	33.3	20.0	21.9
	Scotland	78.4	52.1	63.0	46.5	21.4	25.5

Table 2.25 Source: Regional Trends 38

cantly better results across a range of subjects than the UK averages (Table 2.25). Table 2.24 shows that average weekly earnings are also lower in Scotland compared to the rest of the UK. Both men and women earn around 93% of average UK earnings.

Over 500,000 people in Scotland earn less than £6.50 per hour. This is 30% of all workers. Those working part-time are particularly likely to be low paid. More than half of part-time workers are paid less than £6.50—80% are women. Women make up two-thirds of low paid workers.

Low pay is often combined with job insecurity. In Scotland nearly 50% of men and 33% of women who find work are not in the same job six months later. Low pay also harms pension rights which means that people working in the low pay-no pay cycle will extend their poverty into retirement.

Lower pay, more part-time work and higher unemployment means lower incomes and more poverty in Scotland. More people are dependent on benefits than generally throughout the UK.14% of Scottish households depend on social security benefits for their incomes compared with 12% in the UK as a whole. There are more households in Scotland (19%) receiving Family Credit or Income Support than in the UK (17%), while 19% claim housing benefit and 24% claim council tax benefit in Scotland compared with 15% and 20% for the UK as a whole. As a result of lower incomes fewer people in Scotland have savings. (See Table 2.27.)

There are also more people who are economically inactive due to

Social class of the Working age population (%)

	UK	Scotland
Higher Managerial and Professional	10.8	9.5
Lower Managerial and Professional	22.2	21.9
Intermediate occupations	10.3	10.3
Small employers	7.7	6.0
Lower supervisory	9.4	11.0
Semi-routine	13.3	13.8
Routine	9.8	10.4
Never worked / long-term unemployed	16.5	17.1

Table 2.26 Source: Regional Trends 38

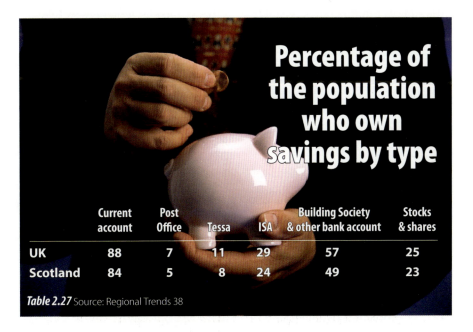

Percentage of the population who own savings by type

	Current account	Post Office	Tessa	ISA	Building Society & other bank account	Stocks & shares
UK	88	7	11	29	57	25
Scotland	84	5	8	24	49	23

Table 2.27 Source: Regional Trends 38

being long-term sick or disabled. In Scotland, 34% of people who are economically inactive are the long-term sick and disabled, some of whom would like to work. The figure for the UK is lower at 27%.

Wealth and poverty sit side by side throughout Scotland as in all the other regions of the UK. Levels of employment, income and deprivation vary significantly between communities which are near neighbours.

Unemployment and economic inactivity are highest in West Central Scotland, which includes Glasgow City, West Dunbartonshire and Inverclyde, and in Dundee City.

Patterns of low pay differ. Rural areas, such as the Scottish Borders, Moray, and Dumfries & Galloway, have the highest levels of low pay. Edinburgh and Aberdeen each have a smaller proportion of their work-force on low pay than elsewhere in Scotland.

Low income, poverty and social ex-clusion are not distributed equally throughout Scotland. The Public Health Institute of Scotland website provides an abundance of informa-tion about the levels of wealth and poverty and their related problems. Table 2.29 compares some of the data from the richest and poorest constituencies in Scotland. One is in Glasgow and one in Edinburgh.

The data illustrates the huge gap between wealth and poverty in small areas of Scotland.

RURAL POVERTY

Poverty is a term usually associ-ated with urban areas. However, poverty exists in rural areas on a scale proportionately as bad as in urban areas but it is not so visible because fewer people are involved.

Lack of access to services, employ-ment and social networks in rural communities is the major cause of social exclusion. Transport is the main problem due to the time and cost involved.

In rural areas, people who need to access support services are very visible. This can be beneficial if it leads to early identification and resolution of the problems. On the other hand, many will hide their problems rather then risk being stigmatised or labelled.

Another problem is deciding which indicators to use to define poverty. In a town, the lack of a car might be used as a minor indicator of poverty. In the country where there is insufficient public transport and large distances to travel, a large proportion of the family budget will be sacrificed to maintain a vehicle. Not having a car then becomes a major indicator of poverty.

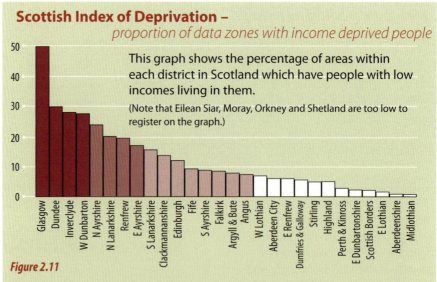

Scottish Index of Deprivation – *proportion of data zones with income deprived people*

This graph shows the percentage of areas within each district in Scotland which have people with low incomes living in them.

(Note that Eilean Siar, Moray, Orkney and Shetland are too low to register on the graph.)

Figure 2.11

In 2004, The Scottish Index of Deprivation showed the extent to which people on low incomes are concentrated in particular geographical areas. Glasgow City has by far the greatest concentration with people on low incomes in 50% of its 700 geographical areas. Dundee, with people on low incomes in 30% of its areas is next, followed by Inverclyde and West Dunbartonshire both of which have 28% of their areas with people on low incomes.

In rural areas the problems of unemployment are made worse by the absence of other possibilities. Should an employee be paid off there is little alternative employ-ment to be found. A person may have to travel a long distance to find other employment. A daily round trip of many miles on roads which may be hazardous if pass-able at all through the winter months makes finding alternative employment very difficult. With fuel at premium prices, long journeys to secure different employment may not be financially viable.

The tourist industry, together with agriculture and its related indus-tries, are important employers in rural Scotland. Both are dominated by low pay and are seasonal in nature. The tourist industry in particular employs people on a seasonal basis. Many employees in these sectors are affected by the no pay-low pay cycle.

Another factor is that in rural Scot-land it is harder for households to have more than one earner. Limited and expensive public transport restricts where people can travel to

Price Indices for Rural Scotland, Aberdeen and Edinburgh

		RURAL SCOTLAND	ABERDEEN	EDINBURGH
Food	1990	105	100	105
	1994	108	100	101
Other goods	1990	115	100	98
	1994	115	100	98
Housing	1990	106	100	103
	1994	86	100	116
Transport	1990	111	100	97
	1994	113	100	96
Services	1990	91	100	101
	1994	91	100	103
ALL	1990	106	100	101
	1994	103	100	103

Table 2.28 Source: *Scottish Rural Life Update 1996*

Health and Wealth Inequalities in two Parliamentary areas of Scotland

Category		Rich Area	Poor Area
Wealth and Income			
Average gross income		£31,478	£17,170
Income support claimants		8%	34%
State benefit / unemployed / low pay		16%	42%
Children in workless households		13%	46%
Average house price		£111,057	£39,539
Owner-occupiers		74%	36%
Household – no car		31%	68%
Adults	– no qualifications	24%	50%
School leaver	– no qualifications	6%	10%
	– Highers	43%	31%
	– to Higher Education	30%	21%
	– to Further Education	20%	29%
Health and Lifestyle			
Life expectancy	– male	76.5	63.9
	– female	81.6	75.9
Proportion of 15-year-olds reaching 65	– males	83.6%	54.7%
	– females	91.0%	77.7%
Death Rates / 100,000 of the population			
	– Heart	92	182
	– Stroke	43	68
	– Lung cancer	33	74
	– Drug related	42	153
	– Smoking	351	987
Long-term limiting illness		16%	32%
Self-assessed – health not good		7%	21%
Adults unable to work due to disability		7%	28%
Smokers		30%	50%
Smoked during pregnancy		23%	36%
Obese	–male	63%	56%
	– female	51%	53%
	– pre-school children	24%	21%
Alcohol (excess of weekly recommended intake)	– male	32%	38%
	– female	19%	13%
Teenagers – hospital treatment related to alcohol		0.6/100	1.1/100
Exercise	– male	40%	34%
	– female	30%	24%
Daily fruit consumption	– male	48%	38%
	– female	62%	52%
Teenage pregnancies		4.7/100	7.2/100
Lone Parent Households		15%	35%

Table 2.29 Source: Public Health Institute of Scotland Website (Most figures have been rounded.)

find work. If the family car is being used by the main breadwinner, others will find it difficult to access a second job.

Where childcare facilities exist, people may have to travel long distances to access them which does not make them viable due to time and cost. In urban areas many households escape poverty because more than one adult is working. Rural living makes this less likely.

The higher cost of living in rural areas increases poverty. Food, housing and transport costs are all higher in rural areas. (See Table 2.28.) People have to travel considerable distances to access services such as hospitals, dentists, chemists, petrol stations, schools and shops. With transport so expensive and up to one-third of people not having a car, many are forced to use the local shop where prices are higher and choice more restricted.

The cost and availability of housing is another problem. Hidden homelessness is common. People are forced to live with friends or relations for extended periods of time. Some are seasonally homeless. They can rent caravans or holiday homes over the winter months but cannot afford the tourist season rental rates.

Social housing has always been a problem in rural communities and was made worse by the right to buy legislation. There was a higher proportion of the housing stock sold in rural areas than in the towns. The market for holiday homes has pushed prices up beyond the pockets of many rural people. So even when people can get a job they might not be able to find affordable accommodation nearby.

Tied housing is also a problem. In the most remote areas, employers may offer a house along with a job to attract employees. However, it means that the employer may offer low wages to offset the accommodation that is on offer and it also leads to insecurity. Employees know that if they lose their job they will also lose their house.

Chapter 3

Gender inequalites

In the twentieth century dramatic changes occurred in the economic and social position of women in UK society. However, despite these changes women have yet to achieve equality.

SOCIAL CHANGE

Society is changing. People's living arrangements changed significantly in the last quarter of the twentieth century. Only about 50% of men and women live as married couples. One in ten men and women now cohabit. Over 20% of women and nearly 30% of men never marry and live on their own. There are more than three times as many widows as widowers because women tend to live longer.

The average age at marriage for both men and women in England and Wales rose by seven years between 1971 and 2001 to nearly 35 years of age for men and 32 years for women. Women are waiting longer to have children. In 1971, the average age for a woman to have her first child was 23.7 but by 2004 it was 27.1.

Divorce is increasing. There were 1.5 million divorced men and 2.0 million divorced women in 2001, compared with 1971 when there were 187,000 men and 296,000 women who were divorced.

The number of lone parent households has increased rapidly. In 1971, lone parent families accounted for 4% of all family groups in the UK but this had trebled to 12% in

2005. Until the mid-1980s most of the increase was due to divorce, but recently it has been due to the rise in the proportion of births outside marriage. In 1980, 12% of all children born were to women who were not married. In 2004 the figure was 42%.

Currently, lone parent families account for 25% of families with dependent children. The majority of families with dependent children (63%) are still headed by married couples, while 12% are cohabiting couples. Lone mothers head 90% of lone parent families with just one in ten headed by a lone father.

These changes have had an impact on the income and wealth of women and children.

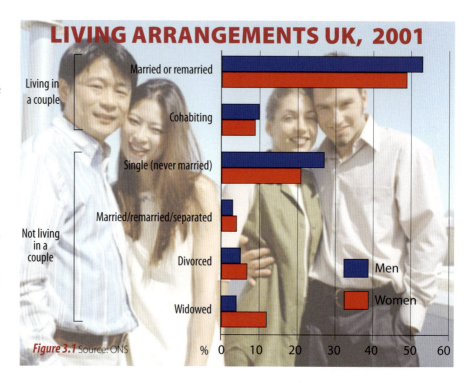

LIVING ARRANGEMENTS UK, 2001

Living in a couple
- Married or remarried
- Cohabiting

Not living in a couple
- Single (never married)
- Married/remarried/separated
- Divorced
- Widowed

Men
Women

% 0 10 20 30 40 50 60

Figure 3.1 Source: ONS

People in households by type of household and family (%)

	1971	2005
One person	6	12
One family households:		
Couple		
No children	19	25
Dependent children	52	37
Non-dependent children only	10	9
Lone parent	4	12
Other households	9	5

Table 3.1 Source: Census, Labour Force Survey, Office for National Statistics

WOMEN'S ECONOMIC ROLE

The proportion of women in the workforce grew from 29% in 1900 to 46% in 2000 which represents an increase from 5 million to 13 million. Since 1975, the employment rates for women have increased while those for men have been falling. (See Table 3.2.) In 1983

UK Employment rates by gender (%)

	1975	2005
Women	59.5	70.1
Men	90.1	79.0

Table 3.2 Source: Labour Force Survey

men were employed in 2.5 million more jobs than women. By 2003 there were almost the same number of men and women in jobs—13 million for men and 12.8 million for women—but almost half of the female jobs were part-time. Women make an increasingly important contribution to the income of families with children. Women are the main, and frequently the only, breadwinner in lone parent families. In two parent families the woman's economic contribution often makes the difference between living in poverty or not.

Families with only one parent working are over four times more likely to have incomes in the bottom 20% than those families where both parents are working full-time. (See Table 3.3.) In families where both parents work, even if one only works part-time, still only 4% have incomes in the bottom 20% of incomes. When only one parent works, 17% are in the bottom quintile.

Women are more likely to be poor than men

On average women have lower incomes than men. They work in lower paid sectors of the economy, are less likely to reach the top in their chosen careers and are more likely to work in part-time jobs or depend on benefits because they are lone parents. (See Table 3.4.)

Net disposable incomes after housing costs
2003 / 2004 (%)

	Bottom quintile	Second quintile	Middle quintile	Fourth quintile	Top quintile
Couple in full-time work	4	8	19	32	37
Couple, one full-time, one part-time	4	19	29	26	22
Couple, one working one not working	17	27	23	16	17
Unemployed	76	12	7	3	2

A quintile is 20% so these figures divide household incomes into groups of 20%
Table 3.3 Source: DWP, Households Below Average Income 2003–04

Net disposable incomes after housing costs
2003 / 2004 (%)

	Bottom quintile	Second quintile	Middle quintile	Fourth quintile	Top quintile	Individuals (millions)
Pensioner couple	19	27	22	17	15	7.1
Single pensioner:						
Male	12	33	21	18	16	1.1
Female	19	37	21	16	9	3.2
Couple, with children	19	22	23	20	16	19.6
Single with children	46	23	16	11	4	4.9

A quintile is 20% so these figures divide household incomes into groups of 20%
Table 3.4 Source: DWP, Households Below Average Income 2003–04

Women continue to be placed in the traditional role of carer for children, the elderly, the sick and the disabled. This places them at a financial disadvantage because they take career breaks or work part-time or live on welfare. In addition, the extra costs of funding those who need to be cared for are costs that women share so they have less to spend on themselves. Even in two parent relationships, women bear a greater burden of the cost of children.

Finally, women live longer. A life lived in poverty continues on beyond retirement age. There are more elderly women in the UK than men and many more women depend on means-tested benefits because they did not have careers that enabled them to earn pension rights. There are three times as many single female pensioners as there are male and more live on lower incomes. (See Table 3.4.)

Women earn less

In 2004 men in full-time jobs had average earnings of £24,236. Women, by contrast, had average earnings of £18,531 which is about 24% less. Pay differentials vary by region. The largest difference was in London, where men with an average income of £39,022 earned 35% more than women on £28,833.

Men Earn More

London	35%
East Midlands	32%
South-east	32%
North-west	30%
South-west	30%
Scotland	29%
East of England	29%
Yorkshire and Humberside	26%
West Midlands	24%
Wales	21%
North-east	19%
Northern Ireland	15%

Table 3.5

In part-time work women earn over 40% less than men.

The gender pay gap also varies from industry to industry with the biggest differential being in banking and finance and the smallest in agriculture and forestry. (See Table 3.6.)

WHY DO WOMEN EARN LESS?

Table 3.7 illustrates that discrimination remains the main reason for gender pay differentials. This is followed by less full-time employment experience and interruptions to being in the labour market for family reasons. Segregation, with women working in lower paid sectors of the economy, is another important component.

Full-time earnings by sector 2004 (hourly rates)

United Kingdom Industry sectors	Women (£)	Men (£)	pay gap (%)
Banking, insurance & pension provision	13.61	24.23	44
Health & social work	10.87	15.50	30
Other community, social & personal service	10.49	14.53	28
Real estate, renting & business activities	12.07	16.03	25
Wholesale, retail & motor trade	8.87	11.72	24
Electricity, gas & water supply	12.35	15.38	20
Manufacturing	10.09	12.49	19
Public administration & defence	10.99	13.52	19
Hotels & restaurants	7.09	8.13	13
Construction	10.45	11.84	12
Education	13.30	14.97	11
Transport, storage & communication	11.18	12.15	8
Agriculture, hunting & forestry	7.64	7.76	2

Table 3.6 Source: ONS (2004) Annual Survey of Hours and Earnings 2004

Components of pay gap per hour worked

COMPONENT	% GAP
Years of full-time employment experience	26
Interruptions to the labour market due to family care	15
Years of part-time employment experience	12
Education	6
Segregation	13
Discrimination and other factors associated with being female	29
Total	100

Table 3.7 Source: Women and Equality Unit

Percentage of workers in industry sectors by gender

	Females	Males
Agriculture, hunting, forestry and fishing	0.6	1.3
Construction	1.3	7.6
Distribution, hotels and catering, repairs	26.5	22.1
Education, social work and health services	30.3	8.4
Electricity, gas, water	0.3	0.8
Financial and business services	19.0	20.2
Manufacturing	7.8	20.2
Mining, quarrying, (inc oil and gas extraction)	0.1	0.5
Public administration and defence	5.2	5.2
Transport, storage and communication	3.4	8.8
Other	5.5	5.0
Whole economy (thousands)	12,460 (=100%)	12,996 (=100%)

Table 3.8 Source : Social Trends

Women work in the lower paid sectors of the economy

Men and women work in different areas of the economy and within these they are found in different occupations. Women are over-represented in areas of the economy which are low paid. Nearly two-thirds of women are employed in twelve occupation groups. (See Table 3.9.) These are sometime described as the five 'c's—caring, cashiering, catering, cleaning and clerical occupations.

78.3% of those working in education, social work and health services are women and they are also well represented in catering and in offices dealing with cash, marketing and sales, and personnel. These sectors have been traditionally lower paid than equivalent skilled work in other areas of the economy.

Table 3.9 shows that more than twice as many men as women are in the higher and professional occupations in the UK. In other words,

in occupations where women are over-represented, men tend to have the higher managerial positions.

Over the last ten years women have experienced some improvement because of structural changes in the economy. The service sector is growing. Women are found in increasing numbers in occupations previously dominated by men. 75% of pharmacists, 33% of medical practitioners, nearly half of all lawyers and nearly 40% of

UK Occupational segregation 2004
Selected occupations
Employees and self-employed aged 16 and over (%)

	Women	Men
Receptionists	95	5
Nurses	88	12
Care assistants & home carers	88	12
Primary & nursery teachers	87	13
General office assistants or clerks	83	17
Cleaners & domestics	80	20
Financial clerks & bookkeepers	77	23
Retail cashiers & check-out operators	77	23
Kitchen & catering assistants	73	27
Customer care	72	28
Sales & retail assistants	71	29
Office managers	67	33
Secondary teachers	54	46
Chefs & cooks	46	54
Retail & wholesale managers	35	65
Marketing & sales managers	26	74
ICT managers	18	82
Software professionals	17	83
Production, works & maintenance managers	9	91

Table 3.9

Socio-economic classification:
by gender, 2005 (%)

	Males	Females
Higher managerial and professional occupations	15	7
Lower managerial and professional occupations	20	24
Intermediate occupations	5	15
Small employers and own account workers	11	4
Lower supervisory and technical occupations	12	5
Semi-routine occupations	10	16
Routine occupations	11	7
Never worked and long-term unemployed	15	21

Table 3.10 Source: Social Trends 36

all accountants are now female. The proportion of female managers and senior officials increased from under 10% in the early 1990s to one-third in 2005. Increasing numbers of women, then, are entering occupations offering higher earnings.

However, even in the new industries there are several areas where women are poorly represented. Women account for only 14% of the professionals in science and technology while the number of female professionals in information and communications technology is actually falling.

Lower pay for same work

Gender pay differentials still remain. For example, the median hourly earnings of full-time female medical practitioners are 23% less than male earnings. Female legal professionals earn 21% less, and female accountants earn 15% less than males in these professions.

Men start to earn more as soon as they enter the job market and the gender earnings gap widens with age. Women aged 18–21 earn 2% less than men, but those aged 40–49 earn 20% less. Women get fewer qualifications, skills, and work experience because they are more likely to take career breaks to care for children.

Females entering the labour market have higher qualifications than males, whereas thirty years ago men had better qualifications than women. Recent research indicates that education and experience is equal between men and women at the outset of their careers so the gender pay gap is small. However, after ten years in the job market, despite working continuously full-time, a woman's income is 12% less than a man's. Part of the difference may be explained by men and women entering different occupations but the major cause is discrimination.

Interruptions to work experience

Although women now have higher qualifications than men, they are more likely to work part-time or take time out of work to care for children. Therefore they have less access to training than men and gain less work experience. Experience is one of the factors that employers reward and it is often difficult for women to return to work at the same level or at a higher level after taking time out.

After a long period out of work women face barriers to returning such as low confidence and outdated skills. Even after a relatively short time it can be difficult for women to find jobs that match their skills, particularly if the work they want to find is local or part time.

A low skilled mother of two, taking time out to care for her children, loses £250,000 in earnings over her lifetime. A mid skilled woman would lose 26% or £140,000 and a high skilled woman would lose 2% or £20,000. A mid skilled mother of two who started her family when she was 24 would lose twice as much as much as she would if she had waited until she was 30.

33

Lower income means fewer pension contributions so women face reduced circumstances when they are old.

Part-time work

Many more women than men work part-time. Women are most likely to work part-time when they are caring for young children. Those who have children under 11 are the group most likely to work part-time (See Table 3.11.) Approximately two-thirds of women with children under the age of 11 work part-time, compared to only one-third of women with no dependent children. Only one mother in ten remains in full-time continuous work following the birth of her first child.

Parents' employment
2004 in percentages

	Dependent children aged		
	0–4	5–10	11+
Women			
Employment rate	52	71	77
Working part-time	65	65	48
Men			
Employment rate	90	90	89
Working part-time	4	4	4

Table 3.11
Source: Equal Opportunities Commission website

Women tend to work part-time between the ages of 25 and 45. These are the main child rearing years but are also the prime years of their career. Men, on the other hand, mostly work part-time when they are students or when they are winding down to retirement. Research has shown that women working part-time for just one year during the prime of their career can expect to earn 10% less after fifteen years than a woman who never worked part-time.

Women who work part-time earn 32% less per hour than women working full-time and 41% less than men working full-time. Part of the reason is that women working part-time have lower educational

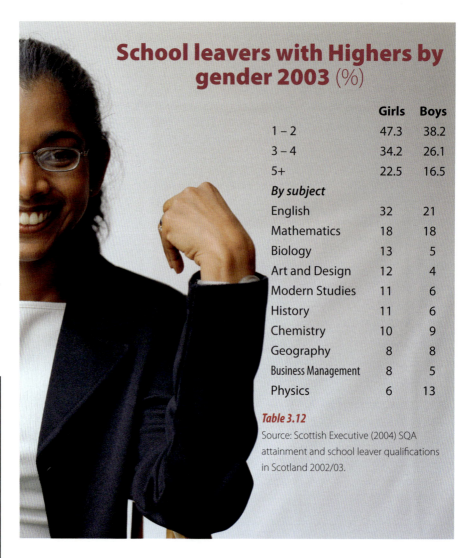

School leavers with Highers by gender 2003 (%)

	Girls	Boys
1 – 2	47.3	38.2
3 – 4	34.2	26.1
5+	22.5	16.5
By subject		
English	32	21
Mathematics	18	18
Biology	13	5
Art and Design	12	4
Modern Studies	11	6
History	11	6
Chemistry	10	9
Geography	8	8
Business Management	8	5
Physics	6	13

Table 3.12
Source: Scottish Executive (2004) SQA attainment and school leaver qualifications in Scotland 2002/03.

levels than those who work full-time. However, the main reason is that part-time work is concentrated in lower paid jobs.

One in four women working part-time are retail sales assistants, cleaners or care assistants. Few work as managers. In order to find work at times that suit childcare, many women have to change their employer and their occupation and take a pay cut.

Time taken to travel to and from work is also an issue. Women with children often need to live closer to their place of work because they also have to access childcare. Alternatively, they may only be able to travel a short distance because they have to fit work and travel into the time when their children are at school or nursery. This limits the range of jobs available to them.

WOMEN, EDUCATION AND INCOME

Females have overtaken males in educational qualifications. Table 3.12 shows that girls leave school with better qualifications than boys and, with the exception of physics, they outperform boys in most subjects.

More girls are now going on to university and higher education than boys. Females now outperform males at both undergraduate and postgraduate levels. In 2003–04, just under 60% of higher education qualifications were obtained by women.

It would be reasonable to assume that there would be no difference in pay rates between highly educated men and women in the early years of work. At this stage the level of pay is a reward for specific qualifications, not experience. However, women earn 15% less than men

Women's representation in the public & voluntary sectors

Women make up:

- 38.6% of public appointments
- 12.4% of local authority chief executives
- 0.8% of senior ranks in the armed forces
- 8.3% of senior police officers
- 24.4% of civil service top management
- 45.4% of chief executives of voluntary organisations
- 8.3% of top judges (high court judge & above)
- 30.5% of secondary school head teachers
- 27.4% of FE college principals
- 15.0% of university vice chancellors
- 27.7% of health service chief executives
- 16.9% of trade union general secretaries or equivalent
- 16.7% of heads of selected professional bodies

Table 3.13

Source: EOC: Sex and power: who runs Britain? (2005)

The Glass Ceiling refers to the invisible barriers which prevent women reaching the top of their chosen careers.

only three years after graduation, so the pay difference is significant right from the start. The gender pay gap for young graduates might be explained in part by male and female graduates entering different occupations.

The subjects boys and girls choose will influence their careers. At A level, girls are well represented in subjects such as English, psychology, art and design, sociology, biology and the expressive arts/drama, while boys choose physics, mathematics, economics, computing and business studies. Similarly in Scotland, girls choose different subjects from boys. (See Table 3.12.)

School subject choice influences higher education subject choice. Few women study science subjects. They account for only 14% of engineering and technology students, 24% of computer science students and 22% of those studying physics. More males study finance, economics and politics. These are subjects which can lead to well-paid careers.

More women than men study social science subjects such as history, and arts subjects such as languages. These generally lead to jobs in less well-paid sectors of the economy. However, nearly 70% of students of medicine and dentistry are women.

Nevertheless, even where men and women enter the same occupation with the same qualifications there is a salary gap.

THE GLASS CEILING

The term the 'glass ceiling' was first used in the 1980s to describe the invisible barrier that stops women (and other disadvantaged groups) reaching the top in their chosen career. It is usually applied to barriers to senior management positions.

The glass ceiling is created in a number of informal ways.

- ✳ Women, as the main carers, take career breaks which prevent career development.
- ✳ It is difficult for women to access male-dominated networks based on after-hours socialising in the pub and at the golf club. These networks can influence appointments and promotion.
- ✳ 'Presenteeism' is the idea that senior management must be seen working long hours. There is a lack of part-time work and flexible working at senior levels.
- ✳ Stereotyping and discrimination. Male directors may develop prejudices about a woman's commitment and ambitions – particularly the idea that having children is incompatible with senior roles.
- ✳ Lack of role models. There are very few female role models in senior positions to dispel these stereotypes and to inspire women to move into senior levels.

Table 3.13 shows that women are very much in the minority in top posts in the UK. Barely one-third of all managers and senior officials are women and they tend to be in the lower paid areas of management. For example, 60% of personnel and marketing managers,

35

whose median pay is less than £19 per hour, are women, but only 26% of corporate managers and senior officials, whose median pay is over £39 per hour, are women.

According to women, the main barrier preventing them taking on senior roles is the lack of quality part-time work. The prevailing male belief in presenteeism at the top levels of business prevents this. Yet there are some companies that are beginning to make changes and have seen the benefits of them.

MSN UK (Microsoft) introduced a project to move away from long hours and presenteeism when it opened up flexible working for all staff. It began by retraining its senior managers. The business has benefited from improved morale and staff retention and 81% of staff believe they provide a better service and meet their objectives because they work flexibly.

The number of women who are starting up their own companies is on the increase. There are now 46 women for every 100 men starting their own enterprises and the gap narrows every year. Women are choosing to give up guaranteed salaries, bonuses, pensions, health insurance, etc. for the risk, hard work and uncertainty of their own

Michelle Mone (above) is an example of a successful businesswoman. She developed a very succesful underwear business which now sells its products in markets around the world.

enterprise. The benefit is the opportunity to work flexibly.

Therefore the idea that women do not get promotion in established companies because they do not have enough drive is not correct or women would not be taking the risks to start their own businesses. The failure of established businesses to promote women is for reasons other than ability and ambition.

The glass ceiling in education

In primary schools, 82% of teachers are women yet nearly half of primary heads are men. In secondary teaching women account for nearly half of the teachers but only 30% of headteachers are women.

In higher education women account for 40% of academics but only 30% of department heads. Women are more likely to be offered fixed term contracts rather than a staff job. 48% of women are on fixed term contracts compared to only 38% of men. Only 13% of professors in older universities are women.

Therefore in all areas of life women are still faced with obstacles to advancement and promotion in their chosen career.

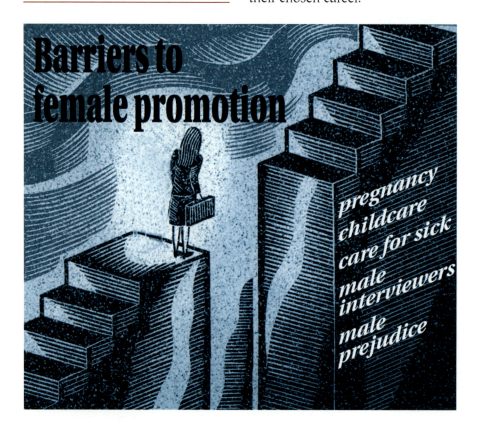

LONE PARENTS

In the UK 25% of families are lone parent families—1.7 million parents with 2.9 million dependent children. Nine out of ten lone parents are lone mothers. In Scotland there are 162,000 lone parent families with over 280,000 children.

Marital Status

	Lone Mothers	Lone Fathers
Divorced	33%	43%
Separated	24%	30%
Single	38%	13%
Widowed	6%	14%

Table 3.14

Source: One Parent Families Scotland

Ten percent of lone parents are under 25, while 55% are in the age group 25 – 44. As Table 3.14 shows, most become lone parents through separation and divorce which is the reason for most lone parents being in this older age group.

Lone parent families are particularly vulnerable to poverty. Most lone parent families with one child have an income of between £100 and £200 per week compared with £800 to £900 for similar two parent families. In Scotland 70% of lone parent families have an income of less than £10,000 per year compared to only 25% of two parent families. 79% of single parents have no savings compared to 41% of two parent families.

In 2005 the employment rate for lone parents was 55.5% which was an increase of over 5% since 2000. This is an indication that government policies designed to get lone parents into work are having some success. However, the employment rate for lone parents is much lower than for mothers who are married or cohabiting. The reason for the difference is childcare. Where there are two parents one can be looking after the family while the other is out at work.

In Sweden 70% of lone mothers work and in France the figure is 82%. In France and Sweden there

Childcare arrangements for children with working mothers: by age of child, 2003 (%)[1]

	Formal childcare	Informal childcare[2]	Childcare not required
0–2	42	64	10
3–4	43	64	13
5–7	23	67	24
8–10	20	65	28
11–13	5	52	46
14–16	1	18	82

Table 3.15 Source: Families and Children Study, Department for Work and Pensions
1 Percentages do not add up to 100% as respondents could give more than one answer.
2. Provided by partners, parents, friends, and older children.

is far more affordable childcare available for single parents. In the UK, The Childcare Cost Survey for the Day Care Trust found that a full-time nursery place for a child under 2 typically costs over £7,000 per year.

Ninety percent of lone parents say they would like to find paid employment but face barriers. They identify the main one as the cost and availability of childcare. Table 3.15 shows that working mothers mainly depend on informal arrangements for looking after their children.

The childcare element of Working Tax Credit enables lone parents to get up to 70% of their childcare

costs, up to £100 per week for one child. Nevertheless, even with this assistance the cost of childcare can make a lone mother poorer if she goes out to work.

Another problem is that many lone parents have limited qualifications

Ownership of selected items

Item	Single Parent Families	Two Parent Families
Car	33%	86%
Telephone	88%	98%
Computer	24%	54%
Internet Access from Home	6%	26%

Table 3.16

Source: One Parent Families Scotland

or skills. A survey for the Department of Social Security reported that 50% of lone parents had no educational qualifications, compared with 38% of all women aged 25–49. The same survey found that 76% of unemployed lone parents had no vocational training.

When lone parents find work it is often low paid so they merely replace workless poverty with working poverty. The government has introduced tax credits to help boost the income of low paid single parents in work. However, even in this system there are problems. In 2003 – 04, 2 million tax credits were overpaid of which 353,000 were to lone parents. The vast majority of these overpayments were due to mistakes made by the Inland Revenue. The demands for repayment left many lone parent families with incomes below the Income Support level.

Many lone parent families depend on benefits for their income. 52% of lone parents in Scotland claim Income Support. With Income Support levels below the HBAI rate, the majority of lone parent families claiming benefit live in poverty.

The proportion of lone parents in income poverty in Scotland fell from 56% in the mid-1990s to 47% in 2003 – 04. This is almost three times the rate for couples with children. It includes both lone parents who are working and lone parents who are not. Around half are working and half are not. Therefore lone parents have a high risk of living in poverty whether they are in work or not.

Lack of income has an impact on living standards and health. Children in lone parent families are much more likely to go without necessities than children in two parent families. Table 3.16 shows the wide gap in levels of ownership of certain items between single parent families and two parent families.

Survey by *lone-parents.org*

	Yes	No
Do you prefer being a lone parent?	35%	65%
Do you suffer from anxiety or panic attacks?	42%	58%
Do you have a problem sleeping?	94%	6%
Do you often buy yourself new clothes?	30%	70%
Would you say that your children are at a disadvantage in any way?	48%	52%
Are you happy?	46%	54%
Do you usually have a holiday away with the kids?	7%	93%
Do you ever cry for no apparent reason?	61%	39%
Has the CSA done anything that helps you in any way?	12%	88%
Do you have a car?	65%	35%
Do you have any close friends that you can lean on?	63%	37%

Table 3.17
Source: www.lone-parents.org.uk

In housing, lone parents in Scotland are more dependent on rented housing and are more likely to live in a flat. Only 25% of lone parents live in owner-occupied housing compared to 71% of two parent families. Lone parent families tend to move more often than two parent families. 41% of lone parent families have lived in their current home for two years or less compared to 24% for two parent families.

Despite these differences research has shown that lone parents spend almost as much on their children as married parents. To do this mothers spend considerably less on themselves, including frequently going without food. This has a major impact on their health.

Lone mothers report poor health and limiting long-standing illness almost twice as often as mothers living with a partner. Table 3.17 illustrates that lone mothers suffer from stress as a consequence of being on their own as well as from living in poverty. Stress, poverty and depriving oneself of food make lone parents more likely to suffer from ill-health.

WOMEN'S TRADITIONAL ROLE AS CARER

Over the past twenty years women who have young children, more than any other group, have been steadily increasing their participation in the workforce. The Labour Force Survey in 2005 showed that 56% of women of working age whose youngest child is under 5 are currently employed, compared to 91% of men. Women who have children tend to drop out of the labour market. However, those who

(continued on page 40)

THE BURDEN OF BEARING THE COST OF CHILDREN

Whatever the structure of the family, women tend to bear a greater burden than men of the cost of bringing up children. Women experience poverty in different ways from men because the responsibility for managing household poverty usually falls on women.

Changes in household income affect men and women in different ways. A study for the Scottish Poverty Information Unit in areas of high deprivation examined the ways that women in low income families managed the resources available to their families and themselves and the effect this had on their wellbeing.

An increase in a woman's income means that the whole family benefits from the extra spending power. A fall in household income, on the other hand, was borne initially by the woman on her own through a reduction in her personal spending. Women felt that encouraging their partners to give up some personal spending was likely to cause conflict in the family.

Men tend to act in the opposite manner. An increase in income means that personal spending tends to increase, while a reduction in income is often passed on to the family for the woman to deal with before personal spending is reduced.

The majority of women see the well-being of their children as their major family priority. It often means that debt management becomes a daily, as well as a long-term, problem for women. Debt is often necessary to even out spending over a period of time but it is kept hidden from their partners.

Women discuss debt problems and look for support from female family and friends. Loans are usually obtained from female family and friends. Loans are given or sought to buy children's clothes, pay fuel bills and for items of household equipment. Their main priorities are to provide food, rent and fuel for the family.

Normal retail stores are used to buy clothes for older children. However, many women use car boot sales and charity shops for clothes for themselves. Younger children's clothes are either handed down from older brothers or sisters or come from charity shops.

Having to balance low income budgets creates isolation and stress which leads to ill health. The demands made by children,

particularly during the school holidays, cause stress and sleepless nights due to worry.

Christmas is a financial nightmare and is particularly stressful. Being unable to buy the quality or quantity of food and other goods is a constant reminder of their social exclusion. On the days that low income women are able to shop they are restricted by the type of shop they can enter and the goods they can buy.

Finally, recent research has shown that bearing the main strain of managing poverty has a knock-on effect on the physical and mental health of women which in turn, has an impact on their parenting skills and their ability to find work. There is now a significant body of evidence which shows that the stresses linked to raising children in poverty can make it extremely difficult to provide effective parenting. Parenting support services can help in some cases but they do not address the underlying issue of hardship and the stress it creates.

Making the move from worklessness into work requires the individual to have optimism that it will improve their living standards and wellbeing. However, stress and its impact on health undermines morale and hinders the work of personal advisers in work-focused interviews in New Deal for Lone Parents programmes.

remain in work continue to bear the main responsibility for childcare and domestic work.

The UK Time Use Survey undertaken by the Equal Opportunities Commission found that mothers did 75% of childcare during the week and two-thirds at the weekend. This amounted to two hours each weekday and one and a half hours each Saturday and Sunday. Fathers did around forty five minutes as a daily average through the week and nearly one hour at the weekend.

Mothers also spend over twice as long as fathers doing general household chores like cooking and cleaning during the week. At weekends women do 45% more than men. Trying to combine both care and work is very difficult for many women and creates a great deal of stress. Many mothers are prevented from achieving the work-life balance they desire because of the lack of local part-time work and inadequate childcare provision.

Women are also more likely than men to be carers for elderly or disabled relatives and friends. 11% of the population, almost six million people, provide unpaid care. The proportion of unpaid carers increases as women get older.

Women with these caring responsibilities are much more likely than men to work part-time or not at all, whereas the majority of men with caring responsibilities who do paid work have full-time jobs. This means that women are more likely to have to survive on reduced incomes throughout their lives. At times when they could be earning and contributing to pension rights they are unable do so because of the caring role they adopt or are expected to adopt. Ultimately this means they will continue to live in poverty past retiral age.

WOMEN AND BENEFITS

Women in the UK are twice as likely to live in poverty as men and are more likely to have to depend on benefits. On average, 20% of the incomes for women in the UK are

made up of benefits and tax credits, whereas only 10% of men depend on these for their income. Table 3.18 clearly shows that lone parents have a much greater benefit and tax credit dependency than couples.

One group of welfare-dependent women who are particularly vulnerable are pregnant teenagers. They receive much lower payments than older pregnant women. The majority of teenagers who are not living at home have less than £20 each week to spend on food, so they live on cheap foodstuffs such as chips, biscuits and sweet breakfast cereals which are high in fat and sugar. Babies born to teenagers tend to have lower birth weights, with an

Receipt of selected social security benefits among families below pension age: by type of benefit, 2003/04

	Single person with dependent children (%)	Couple with dependent children (%)
INCOME-RELATED		
Council tax benefit	48	8
Housing benefit	45	7
Working tax credit or income support	46	5
Jobseeker's allowance	1	2
Any income-related benefit	56	10
NON-INCOME-RELATED		
Child benefit	97	97
Incapacity or disablement benefits	8	9
Any non-income-related benefit	97	97
Any benefit or tax credit	98	98

Table 3.18 Source: Family Resources Survey, Department for Work and Pensions

Current pension scheme membership of employees: by sex and socio-economic classification, 2004–05 (%)

	Managerial and professional	Intermediate	Routine and manual	All
MALE FULL-TIME EMPLOYEES				
Occupational pension	67	63	37	53
Personal pension	27	15	20	23
Any pension	82	68	51	66
FEMALE FULL-TIME EMPLOYEES				
Occupational pension	68	55	34	56
Personal pension	17	15	11	15
Any pension	76	62	40	63
FEMALE PART-TIME EMPLOYEES				
Occupational pension	58	46	25	34
Personal pension	17	13	9	11
Any pension	69	54	32	41

Table 3.19 Source: General Household Survey, Office for National Statistics

increased risk of infant mortality and also an increased risk of health problems in both childhood and later life.

WOMEN LIVE LONGER AND POORER THAN MEN

Table 3.20 shows that women live longer than men. There are 26% more women than men over the age of 60. Looking at those over 80 we find that there are double the number of women. Life expectancy for the UK is 76 years for men and 81 years for women. In Scotland it is lower at 73 for men and 79 for women.

Since working age women on average have lower incomes, the contributions they make are lower and so they have fewer pension rights. More than 80% of women who retire are not entitled to a full basic state pension based on their own contributions. Recent research estimates that women who do not have children and who have middle ranked skills earn £250,000 less over their lifetime than similarly skilled men. For women who have children the difference is much greater.

Table 3.19 shows that women are less likely to have a pension than men, and part-time female workers are the least likely group to gain access to a pension. Lower paid jobs are less likely to have occupational pension schemes. As women are over-represented in these jobs they are less likely to retire with a decent pension and have to rely on mean-tested benefits.

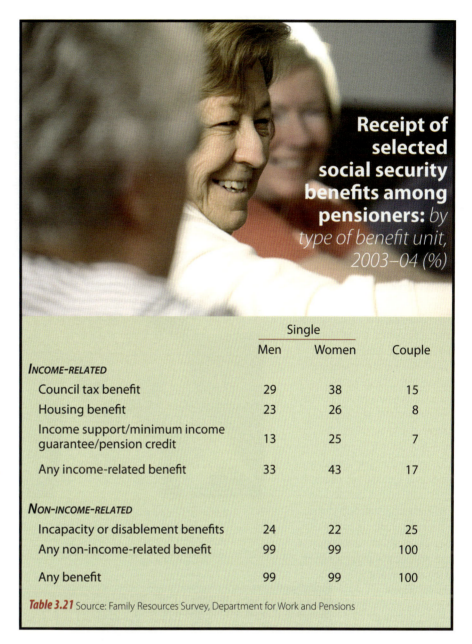

Receipt of selected social security benefits among pensioners: *by type of benefit unit, 2003–04 (%)*

	Single		Couple
	Men	Women	
INCOME-RELATED			
Council tax benefit	29	38	15
Housing benefit	23	26	8
Income support/minimum income guarantee/pension credit	13	25	7
Any income-related benefit	33	43	17
NON-INCOME-RELATED			
Incapacity or disablement benefits	24	22	25
Any non-income-related benefit	99	99	100
Any benefit	99	99	100

Table 3.21 Source: Family Resources Survey, Department for Work and Pensions

As a result, 44% of single female pensioners depend solely on the state retirement pension and have to seek pension credit compared to only 28% of single male pensioners. More males than females have occupational and personal pensions.

More women have to face means-tested benefits in order to survive in their retirement. Table 3.21 illustrates that more single women pensioners are forced to claim council tax benefit, housing benefit, income support and pension credit than men.

In conclusion, women live longer and live poorer than men. Throughout their working lives they are paid less for comparable work. Furthermore, they are more likely to work in low paid employment, work part-time and have long periods when they do not work and may have to live on benefits. With separation, divorce and cohabitation becoming increasingly common, women can no longer depend on husbands or partners to provide for them in their old age. Consequently, far more women face poverty throughout their working lives and for longer in their retirement years because they live longer than men.

Population *by gender and age*
2004 (Millions)

	Males	Females
60–69	2.7	2.8
70–79	1.9	2.3
80 & over	0.8	1.7
Total	5.4	6.8

Table 3.20 Source: Social Trends 36

Equal Pay Act 1970

The *Equal Pay Act* was passed in 1970 and came into effect in 1975. The Act makes it unlawful for employers to discriminate between men and women in pay and conditions such as bonus payments, holidays and sick leave when they are doing the same or similar work, work rated as equivalent, or work of equal value. The Act applies to both men and women.

The Act had an immediate impact. When passed in 1970 the gender pay gap was 37% but by the time it came into effect in 1975, the gap was down to 30%. However, over the subsequent thirty years or more the gap has not been eliminated. Currently the gap in earnings is 24%. While much of that can be accounted for by men and women doing different work, there is evidence to show that women are still being paid less for the same work in many areas.

European law extended the scope of the Act. Even if a man and a woman are earning the same basic pay, the law is breached if other benefits such as a company car, private health care, occupational pension and redundancy payments are not provided on an equal basis.

The struggle for equal pay is on-going. In 2003 new legislation lengthened the time limits for bringing cases and for which arrears payments can be

Barbara Castle was the Labour Cabinet Minister who in 1970 who brought in the Equal Pay Act.

made. As a consequence, local authorities and the NHS faced huge bills for back pay equalisation.

In 2006, Scottish local authorities faced bills of up to £700 million to settle claims for women workers in the public sector such as cleaners and care-at-home staff. An estimated 50,000 women workers in Scotland could claim. In Aberdeen, after a strike which closed fifty schools, the council increased its offer to £15 million. Councils throughout Scotland are having to fund back pay and increase the wages of female staff. Councils in the north-east of England have already paid out more than £100 million to women workers.

Similarly in the NHS, large payments have had to be made. In 2005, the North Cumbria Acute NHS Trust had to pay 1,500 women working at two hospitals in north-west England between £35,000 and £200,000 each after an employment tribunal decided they had suffered pay discrimination since 1991.

The Cumbria trust will have to pay out between £42.5 million and £300 million to its lower paid women nurses, healthcare assistants, clerical officers, sewing machine assistants and telephonists. If similar discrimination can be proved in other NHS trusts, the bill could run into billions of pounds.

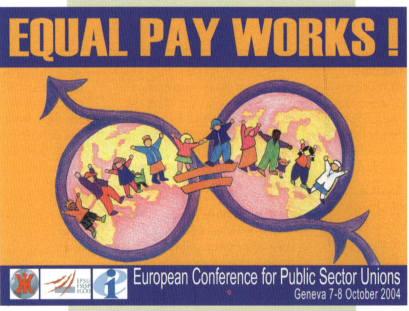

EQUAL PAY WORKS !

European Conference for Public Sector Unions
Geneva 7-8 October 2004

Equal pay is an issue in all industrialised countries. Nordic countries have the best record in equal pay. However, no country has, as yet, achieved gender equality

The EOC can provide expert advice and supports people who need help with a problem involving sex discrimination. It provides advice to help employers create positive equal opportunity management practices and publishes a large number of leaflets and guides for employers.

Thirty years on – is the EOC still needed?

The EOC reported that in 2004 – 05 it "handled nearly 24,000 Helpline calls in the year. The five biggest issues were pregnancy and maternity (21%), equal pay (15%), work-life balance (11%), recruitment and selection (8%), and sexual harassment (6%)." The organisation consulted over 1,000 employers on the issue of pregnancy discrimination and supported several cases in tribunals. They focused on supporting several test cases which would have a large impact on the issues of pregnancy, maternity, flexible working and equal pay.

In Scotland the organisation followed up twelve successful sex discrimination cases which had gone through industrial tribunals to ensure that the organisations concerned were taking steps to prevent future discrimination. In England they followed up seven successful cases to ensure the organisations concerned made changes in their discriminatory policies and practices on the issues of pregnancy, sexual harassment, bullying, flexible working, equal value, family-friendly hours, and sex/race discrimination. They also supported three sexual harassment actions, two of which were successful.

There has been an improvement in the opportunities afforded to both men and women in the UK since the EOC was introduced and the organisation has played a significant part in that improvement. However, as some of the statistics show there are still discriminatory practices in many organisations so the work of the EOC continues to make a valuable contribution to equal opportunities. It will continue to do so if it becomes incorporated into the

Sexual harassment at work is one of the five biggest issues facing the Equal Opportunities Commission

Sex Discrimination Act 1975

The *Sex Discrimination Act* makes it unlawful to discriminate on the grounds of a person's gender. Sex discrimination is not allowed in employment, education, advertising or when providing housing, goods, services or facilities.

The *Sex Discrimination Act* applies to two kinds of discrimination. Direct discrimination means treating someone unfairly because of their gender and indirect discrimination means setting unjustifiable conditions which appear to apply to everyone but in fact discriminate against one gender. Sex discrimina-

tion legislation applies equally to men and women.

Equal Opportunities Commission

The Equal Opportunities Commission (EOC) was set up by parliament in 1976. It aims to eliminate unlawful discrimination on the grounds of gender and to promote equal opportunities for women and men. It monitors legislation and how effective it is and recommends to the government what changes and improvements could be made to the Sex Discrimination and the Equal Pay Acts.

new Commission for Equality and Human Rights (CEHR) which the government plans to establish in 2009.

Child Support Agency

The Child Support Agency (CSA) was introduced in 1993 to try to reduce the cost to the government of paying benefits to nearly 900,000 single parents, most of them mothers, who got little or no maintenance payments from their former partners. Within six months it ran into difficulties and was forced to reopen and reassess around 150,000 cases following complaints from absent fathers that their maintenance payments were too high and from mothers still not receiving any financial support from former partners. Within a year the CSA admitted that it had made calculation errors in 86% of cases.

By 2004, three Chief Executives had been forced to resign following the inability of the CSA to calculate maintenance correctly, collect maintenance from absent parents or pay maintenance that had actually been collected.

In 2003, the CSA's new computer and telephone system was finally introduced at a cost of £456 million—two years late and £56 million over budget. The 1.2 million existing cases could not be transferred onto the new system because it could not cope. In 2004, it

emerged that the number of unprocessed cases stood at 170,000, a figure which was growing by 30,000 per month, and that there were 75,000 cases lost in the system.

In 2005 the CSA admitted that its staff had deliberately entered false information onto the agency's database which caused hundreds of thousands of families to lose income they were owed by both absent parents and the government.

The Liberal Democrats obtained figures which showed that the CSA was owed more than £1 billion in maintenance, two-thirds of which had been written off by 2001. They also found that the CSA delivered on average only £5 maintenance per child per week, of which the Treasury took back a third from mothers on benefit. In one year, over one million phone calls were abandoned as parents give up trying to get through to the CSA.

In a letter to Tony Blair, Frank Field MP wrote: the CSA "now performs worse than it did a year after the

1997 election. Yet the cost of the agency increases. It now costs taxpayers 54p for each pound of maintenance the agency collects. The 2003 reforms, while costing the taxpayer £456 million for the new IT alone, have added to the agency's general chaos and declining performance, and made an intolerably poor service even worse."

In 2006, the government announced a new system would be created to replace the CSA but until that happened the CSA would get another £120 million over three years to improve its performance. Private debt collection agencies would be used to pursue long-standing cases.

Other policies and strategies to deal with gender inequalities in wealth include:
- New Deal
- Working Tax Credit
- Child Tax Credit
- National Minimum Wage
- Welfare Benefits

(See Chapter 5 – Measures to deal with inequalities in wealth.)

Chapter 4

Race inequalities

The ethnic minority population is 8% of the total UK population. It has risen from 3 million in 1991, when it was 5.5% of the population, to 4.6 million people out of a total UK population of 58.7 million. The ethnic minority community consists of a variety of groups each of which have different experiences of wealth and poverty. The largest group is the Asian British of whom those with Indian ancestry form the biggest section. The Pakistani community is the second largest followed by those of mixed race, Black Caribbean and Black African.

The ethnic minority population is not distributed evenly. 96% live in England with only 2% in Scotland, 1% in Wales and fewer than 0.5% in Northern Ireland. In England the majority are concentrated in urban areas such as London, Birmingham and Manchester. 45% of the UK ethnic minority population live in London.

Different groups are concentrated in different regions. The majority of Black Africans (78%), Black Caribbeans (61%) and Bangladeshis (54%) live in London, whereas only 41% of Indians and 32% of Chinese live there.

UK Population: by ethnic group, 2001

	TOTAL POPULATION	
	NUMBER	PERCENTAGE
White	54,153,898	92.1
Mixed	677,117	1.2
Asian or Asian British	2,331,423	4.0
Indian	1,053,411	1.8
Pakistani	747,285	1.3
Bangladeshi	283,063	0.5
Other Asian	247,664	0.4
Black or Black British	1,148,738	2.0
Black Caribbean	565,876	1.0
Black African	485,277	0.8
Other Black	97,585	0.2
Chinese	247,403	0.4
Other ethnic groups	230,615	0.4
All minority ethnic population	4,635,296	7.9
All ethnic groups	58,789,194	100.0

Table 4.1

Growth of the main ethnic minority groups, 1991 and 2001

Great Britain		Thousands
	1991	2001
Indian	865.5	1051.8
Pakistani	491.0	746.6
Bangladeshi	167.8	282.8
Black Caribbean	517.1	565.6
Black African	221.9	484.8
Chinese	162.4	243.3

Table 4.2 Source: Census 2001, Office for National Statistics

COMMUNITY PROFILES

The ethnic minority communities vary in their history and culture. Many of the reasons for wealth and poverty can be explained by these cultural differences.

Indians

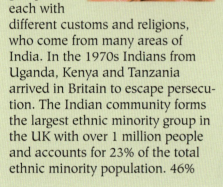

Indians arrived in the UK in large numbers during the 1950s and 1960s to overcome the post-war skill shortages. They were made up of many groups, each with different customs and religions, who come from many areas of India. In the 1970s Indians from Uganda, Kenya and Tanzania arrived in Britain to escape persecution. The Indian community forms the largest ethnic minority group in the UK with over 1 million people and accounts for 23% of the total ethnic minority population. 46% were born in the UK and 75% feel that they have a British national identity. Indians have experienced upward social mobility to a greater extent than other Asian groups. 28% of working age Indians are in a managerial or professional occupation and only 20% are in routine or semi-routine occupations.

Bangladeshis

Most of the Bangladeshi population originates from the north-east of Bangladesh. Male economic migrants arrived in the 1960s and were later joined by their wives and dependants. The Bangladeshi population is currently 283,000 people of whom 46% were born in the UK. However, 82% consider themselves to be British. Bangladeshis are the most economically disadvantaged ethnic minority group with just 11% of the working age population having a managerial or professional occupation and 22% having a routine or semi-routine occupation.

Pakistanis

Large-scale migration from Pakistan has taken place since the 1960s when male economic migrants arrived in the UK. In the 1970s and 1980s the wives and children arrived to join their husbands and fathers. The Pakistani population is 747,000 people. 55% were born in the UK and 83% feel that they have a British national identity. Pakistanis are economically disadvantaged with many more in routine or semi-routine occupations than in managerial or professional positions.

Black Caribbean

A large number of people from the Caribbean migrated to Britain during the 1950s and 1960s in response to the UK government's

(Continued on page 47)

ETHNIC MINORITY GROUPS AND LOW INCOME

A higher proportion of Bangladeshis, Pakistanis and Black non-Caribbeans are living in poverty than any other groups. Table 4.3 shows that all ethnic minority groups are more likely to live in poverty than the White group. The Pakistani and Bangladeshi groups are three times more likely to live in poverty with over half of this group facing poverty.

Most ethnic minority groups, with the exception of the Indian group, earn less than the White British group. In the past many migrants had lower qualifications or had qualifications not recognised in the UK, so many were concentrated in low pay industries such as hotels and catering.

Table 4.4 shows that income inequalities vary by group and also by gender. While black males earn considerably less than white males, black females earn considerably more than white females. Many white females work part-time while more black females work full-time. Both Indian males and females earn more than their white counterparts because they have higher levels of qualifications. (See Table 4.10.)

Risk of being on low income based on ethnic characteristics 2004 – 05

(60% below median income after housing costs)

	Percentage	Nº of individuals in millions
White	18	51.9
Mixed	33	0.4
Indian	30	1.3
Pakistani/Bangladeshi	52	1.1
Black Caribbean	25	0.7
Black Non-Caribbean	45	0.6
Chinese / Other Ethnic Group	36	0.9
All individuals	13	57.1

Table 4.3 Source: DWP

In Scotland, the ethnic groups living in poverty vary slightly from the UK pattern. There are significantly fewer Indians and Chinese in the bottom 40% most deprived group. Only 29% of Indians and 30% of Chinese

advertisements for workers. The current population is 566,000 and is mainly the second and third generation descendants of the original migrants. 58% of Black Caribbeans were born in the UK and 86% consider themselves to be Scots, English or Welsh. The Black Caribbean working age population has seen occupational upward mobility since the 1950s. 28% are now in a managerial or professional occupation which is greater than the 23% in routine or semi-routine occupations. Their occupational structure is similar to that of the white British ethnic group.

Black Africans

The main migration of Black Africans has taken place since the 1970s as a result of political instability in many ex-British colonial African countries. The variety of countries of origin

means that this community has many variations in culture and history. Also, their reasons for migration are varied—political asylum seekers, economic migrants and students.

The Black African population is 485,000. However, because they are mainly recent migrants, only 34% were born in the UK and only 53% think of themselves as having a British identity. Many of this group arrived in the UK with high level skills so 26% are in a managerial or professional occupation while 18% are in a routine or semi-routine occupation.

Chinese

There is a long history of Chinese settlement in the UK, but in the latter part of the twentieth century migration increased and a high proportion of overseas students arrived to study. 243,000 people make up the Chinese population in the UK, of whom only 29% were born in the UK. Nevertheless, 52% consider their national identity to be British. 24% of the working age population are in a managerial or professional

occupation and only 14% are in a routine or semi-routine occupation which is the smallest proportion of any ethnic group. 30% of the working age Chinese population are full-time students and 13% are small employers.

New ethnic minority groups

Over the past fifty years the children of inter-ethnic partnerships have created a population of 674,000. These children are mainly the result of partnerships between people from the White British population and people from various ethnic minority groups. The mixed White and Black Caribbean ethnic group has a population of 237,000, the White and Asian mixed group is 189,000 and the mixed White and African group is 79,000.

Median hourly earnings 2004			
	All	Male	Female
White	£8.00	£9.30	£7.06
Black	£7.33	£7.00	£8.27
Indian	£8.41	£9.56	£7.60
Pakistani / Bangladeshi	£6.25	£6.25	£6.25
Mixed	£7.60	£7.60	£7.58

Table 4.4 Source: Low Pay Commission

Families with dependent children: by ethnic group and family type, 2001			
	Married couple	Cohabiting couple	Lone parent
White	63	12	25
Mixed	42	12	46
Indian	85	2	13
Pakistani	78	3	19
Bangladeshi	79	3	18
Black Caribbean	32	12	57
Black African	44	8	47
Chinese	79	3	18

Table 4.5
Source: Census 2001, Office for National Statistics; Census 2001, General Register Office for Scotland; Census 2001, Northern Ireland Statistics and Research Agency

compared to 42% of White Scots live in deprivation, whereas 48% of Pakistanis and 49% of Bangladeshis fall into this category.

Reasons for inequalities are also cultural. In some groups there is less religious or family pressure to retain the two parent family unit. Black Africans, Black Caribbeans and those in the Mixed group have a higher proportion of lone parent families. Therefore many have to live on benefits or take low paid employment so they and their families live in poverty. (See Table 4.5.)

On the other hand, the poorest groups, Pakistanis and Bangladeshis, are more likely to be married. Pakistani and Bangladeshi women are mainly Muslim and the cultural expectation is for them to stay at home and look after larger families. Table 4.6 shows that three-quarters of Bangladeshi women and over two-thirds of Pakistani women are economically inactive.

The Pakistani and Bangladeshi female populations are relatively young and have a larger proportion of women of childbearing age. 74% of Bangladeshi households and 66% of Pakistani households have dependent children which is a much greater proportion than Indian households with 50% and Black African households with 48%. Only 28% of White British households have dependent children. On average the size of a Pakistani family is 3.4 children and for Bangladeshis it is 3.6, which is significantly larger than the 2.1 children born to the average white woman of childbearing age.

Economic inactivity rates of women: *by ethnic group, 2004*

	Percentages
Bangladeshi	74.7
Pakistani	69.2
Chinese	44.2
Black African	43.2
Mixed	34.4
Indian	33.9
Black Caribbean	26.2
White British	25.2
White Irish	25.1

Table 4.6

Source: Annual Population Survey, Office for National Statistics

Another reason why many women stay at home is that they do not have the high level skills that could command high incomes and in many cases their English is poor which is a major barrier to finding employment.

Unemployment rates of men: by ethnic group, 2004

	Percentages
Black Caribbean	14.5
Black African	13.1
Bangladeshi	12.9
Mixed	12.6
Pakistani	11.0
Chinese	9.7
Indian	6.5
White British	4.5

Table 4.7

Source: Annual Population Survey, Office for National Statistics

UNEMPLOYMENT

Ethnic minority groups have always faced higher rates of unemployment than White British. As Table 4.7 shows, all groups except the Indian group suffer between two and three times the level of unemployment found in the majority population. Indian men had the lowest unemployment rates among the ethnic minority groups, a rate which was only marginally higher than that for White British men.

First generation migrants to the UK would often have several disadvantages which could lead to higher unemployment such as language difficulties, a lack of recognised qualifications and racial prejudice. Some were affected by local economic circumstances because they were concentrated in these areas. For example, the Pakistani community that was concentrated in the North and Midlands of England was badly affected by the closure of manufacturing industries in these areas.

Variations in the unemployment rate may also be a reflection of the different skills and qualifications that each ethnic group possesses. Indian men have low unemployment rates. 30% of them have degree level qualifications whereas relatively few, 15%, have no qualifications. Pakistani and Bangladeshi men have high rates of unemployment. Only 11% and 15% have degree level qualifications, whereas 29% and 40% respectively have no qualifications. Table 4.8 shows that people with qualifications are more likely to be employed than those who have none. The table also shows that there is a significant difference in employment rates between the ethnic minority groups and Whites, whether or not people have qualifications.

In the last ten years all ethnic groups have improved their educational attainment. There are increased numbers of both boys and girls going on to study in universities and colleges. GCSE results in England show Indians and Chinese gaining more passes

Employment rates: by ethnic group and highest qualification, 2004 (%)

	Degree or equivalent	No qualifications
White British	88.7	55.6
Black Caribbean	87.5	48.9
Indian	86.6	49.8
Mixed	85.1	28.8
Black African	78.2	31.1
Pakistani	75.1	28.0
Chinese	66.0	48.4

Table 4.8 Source: Annual Population Survey, Office for National Statistics

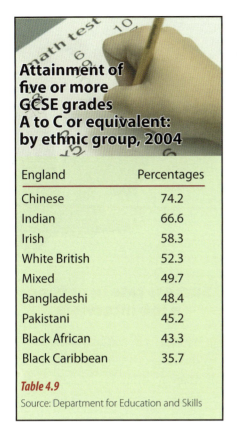

Attainment of five or more GCSE grades A to C or equivalent: by ethnic group, 2004

England	Percentages
Chinese	74.2
Indian	66.6
Irish	58.3
White British	52.3
Mixed	49.7
Bangladeshi	48.4
Pakistani	45.2
Black African	43.3
Black Caribbean	35.7

Table 4.9
Source: Department for Education and Skills

Highest qualification, by ethnic group, in Great Britain, 2001–02

	White British	Black Caribbean	Black African	Indian	Pakistani	Bangladeshi	Chinese
Degree or equivalent (male and female)	15.3	9.5	21.0	22.2	10.7	7.7	23.0
Degree or equivalent (male only)	14.0	11.0	24.0	30.0	11.0	15.0	**
Higher education (below degree level)	8.5	9.1	10.1	5.3	3.0	**	6.2
No qualifications (male only)	14.0	18.0	12.0	15.0	29.0	40.0	**

Table 4.10 Source: Annual Local Area Labour Force Survey, Office for National Statistics

than candidates from the White British ethnic group. (See Table 4.9.) These improvements are mirrored at degree level. The proportion of Chinese, Indians and Black Africans achieving a degree is now significantly higher than for the White British ethnic group.

DISCRIMINATION

Race discrimination in the UK takes three forms—direct discrimination, indirect discrimination and institutional discrimination.

Direct discrimination is when a group of people is treated less favourably on the grounds of race, ethnic origin, religion or belief. Denying someone employment or promotion because they were Asian or Black or White would be direct discrimination.

Indirect discrimination occurs when everyone has to conform to the same practice which would deny a certain group opportunities. For example, if the police were required to wear only standard issue helmets it would indirectly discriminate against Sikhs whose culture re-

quires them to wear a turban. (The police, in fact, issue special turbans as shown on page 54.)

Institutional discrimination occurs when an organisation's procedures and policies disadvantage people from ethnic minority backgrounds. It came to the fore in the Macpherson Report into the Metropolitan Police following the Stephen Lawrence Inquiry. The Report defined it as "the collective failure of an organisation to provide an appropriate and professional service to people because of their colour, culture or ethnic origin. It can be seen or detected in the processes, attitudes and behaviour which amount to discrimination through unwitting prejudice, ignorance, thoughtlessness and racist stereotyping which disadvantage minority ethnic people."

The impact of discrimination on income and living standards

Younger members of ethnic minority populations face fewer barriers than their parents faced. They are fluent in the language, have a better grasp of UK social customs, have

a wider social network and many have made good use of the education system.

However, there still appear to be barriers. For example, 24% of Black African men have a degree level qualification which is a significantly greater number than the 14% of White British males who do. Yet the unemployment rate for Black African men is greater than the unemployment rate for White British men.

Race and religious discrimination may also contribute to the higher unemployment rates of many ethnic minority groups. Although the *Race Relations Act* was introduced in 1968, several studies over the years indicate that discrimination persists. The Home Office Citizenship Survey, published in 2005, reported that individuals from all ethnic minority groups were more likely than those from White ethnic groups to have been refused a job within the previous five years. A significant proportion of those believed they had been refused a job because of their race. Asians also felt that their religion lead to discrimination.

Reasons for being refused a job by ethnic group (%)

	Race	Religion	Colour
White	2	1	1
Asian	20	10	13
Black	27	2	25
Mixed Race	24	**	8

Table 4.11

Source: The Home Office Citizenship Survey 2005

Reasons for being refused promotion by ethnic group (%)

	Race	Religion	Colour
White	5	2	2
Asian	46	16	42
Black	54	4	49
Mixed Race	44	2	31

Table 4.12

Source: The Home Office Citizenship Survey 2005

Percentage of workforce from minority ethnic groups in England and Wales

Police force:	
Police Constables	3
Police Sergeants	2
Inspectors	2
Superintendent and above	2
Prison:	
Prison officer grades	3
Governor grades	2
Probation Service:	
Main grade	10
Senior grades	5
CPS	
Lawyers and administrators	8
Courts	
District judges	4
Circuit judges	1
High Court judges	-

Table 4.13

Source: Race and the Criminal Justice System, Home Office, 2002

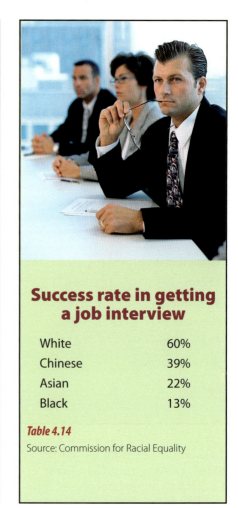

Success rate in getting a job interview

White	60%
Chinese	39%
Asian	22%
Black	13%

Table 4.14

Source: Commission for Racial Equality

Blacks and Asians reported that race and colour were reasons for being refused a job on a high proportion of occasions. On twice as many occasions as Asians, and twenty five times more than White people, Blacks felt that their colour was the reason for not getting a job. Asians felt it was ten times more likely that their race had cost them work than a White person while a Black person felt it was fourteen times more likely. (See Table 4.11.)

Minorities also felt they were denied promotion and advancement in their employment and careers as the result of race or colour discrimination. (See Table 4.12.) Asians also felt that their religion was a discriminatory factor. Muslims in particular, mainly Bangladeshis and Pakistanis, felt that since the events in 2001, their religion was increasingly an issue that denied them jobs and promotion.

In Scotland minorities are underrepresented in the police. Out of 15,963 officers only 118 were recorded as being Black or Asian—107 were constables, 8 sergeants, 2 inspectors and 1 superintendent. In the Lothian and Borders region ethnic minority groups make up 2.5% of the total population, but only 1.1% of the police force. In Strathclyde minority groups are 2.7% of the population, but only 0.8% of police officers—that is about seventy police officers when there should be at least 150 to represent the community. The same applies to every police force area in Scotland, with the exception of Central Scotland Police.

In England and Wales there is a similar picture throughout the Criminal Justice System. Although they are 8% of the population, ethnic minorities are under-represented in almost every area with the exception of the Criminal Prosecution Service and the Probation Service but even here minorities are under-represented in promoted posts. (See Table 4.13.)

Research undertaken by the Commission for Racial Equality attempted to see if people with the same qualifications but with different ethnic backgrounds had similar success rates when applying for jobs. All applicants had different levels of difficulty in getting a job interview, but as Table 4.14 shows Whites had far more success than any other ethnic group. Blacks had by far the worst experience despite having equal or better qualifications and experience. This study demonstrates quite clearly the impact of discrimination in the job market as it exists today in the UK.

RACISM AND RACIST ATTACKS

Racism towards the ethnic minority communities has a major impact on their health, both physically and emotionally. In England and Wales recorded racist incidents are on the increase. Overall they rose by 7% from 49,078 in 2002 – 03 to 52,694 in 2003 – 04. In Scotland, the total number of racist incidents recorded by the police was over 4,800 in 2005 – 06 compared to 4,349 in 2004 – 05. Since the police began recording racist crimes in Scotland

'He terrified me with a knife'

Mohammed Akhtar, who owns a shop in Edinburgh, has been on the receiving end of a string of racist incidents. The most serious was when a youth threatened him last year with a knife while hurling a torrent of racist abuse at him.

Mr Akhtar said: "I told him he couldn't have a free carrier bag and he started shouting at me. He left the shop and then came back in with a knife, calling me a 'greedy Paki bastard' and swearing at me. I picked up the phone to call the police and he ran away. It was terrifying."

There have been several other occasions when racists have come into his shop shouting the all too familiar insults. "People come in telling me to get back to my own country. I have a beard and people taunt me and call me a terrorist. "They shout the same things: 'You black bastard' and 'Go home Paki'. I have had my windows smashed because I am Asian. It makes me so angry.

"Things have definitely got worse since the 1980s. We get more now since 9/11 and especially after the Tube bombs. "The police are very good and do as much as they can, but you are left feeling so annoyed."

Mr Khan, a member of Edinburgh Pakistan Society and the city's police board, also believes attacks on Muslims have increased since the terror attacks in London and New York.

Edited extract from *Call for action in schools as racist crime in Scotland hits all-time high*, Scotsman 21 March 2006

in 2000, the number of incidents has risen by 75%.

Part of this increase may be explained by a greater willingness on the part of victims to report these crimes. However, many organisations which represent ethnic minorities say that most incidents go unreported because the ethnic minorities have no confidence in the police. The clear-up rates are poor (see Table 4.15) and with so few ethnic minorities in the police force the communities do not feel adequately represented. A report by the Commission for Racial Equality Scotland stated:

"Verbal abuse ... was so much a part of everyday life that most people do not think of reporting it."

Many of these attacks are concentrated in poorer areas of cities where many disadvantaged ethnic minorities live. So, many who are forced by low income to live in such areas become the target of racist abuse and violence the perpetrators of which are mostly youths. Nevertheless, racism and racist violence spills over into all areas of our cities and affects ethnic minorities at all economic levels.

The consequence of this is the physical violence faced by many minorities. There were 52,694 racially aggravated crimes in 2003 – 04. Of these 14% were for wounding and 11% for assault. There were twenty two homicides identified as having a "known racial motivation." Twelve victims were White, four Asian, three Black and three other. The rest of the crimes were criminal damage (16%) and harassment, a high proportion of which takes place in or near the victim's home or property.

On top of this are the emotional effects of having to face harassment in its many forms on a regular basis and the fear of living in a community in which unprovoked violence can erupt at any time. (See 'He terrified me with a knife').

In one study, undertaken in several cities including Glasgow, research-

Racially aggravated offences recorded by police in England and Wales by offence and detection rate (%)

	Harassment	Other wounding	Criminal damage	Common assault	Total
Incidents which were racially aggravated	13.4	1.6	0.6	2.2	1.8
Racially aggravated incidents which were cleared up	40.0	40.0	18.0	33.0	34.0
Non-racially aggravated offences cleared up	70.0	55.0	13.0	48.0	28.0

Table 4.15

Source: Statistics on race and the criminal justice system. A Home Office publication under Section 95 of the Criminal Justice Act 2003

ers used in-depth interviews to study people who had been victims in or near their homes. It is particularly stressful for someone to feel insecure in their own home and can lead to severe physical and emotional problems.

The researchers found that the volume of racist experiences was so great that it was sometimes difficult for individuals to isolate specific incidents. The worst offenders were children and youths, with the main victims also being children and youths in the minority communities. Most parents of the perpetrators were racists themselves and supported their offspring.

The racist attacks reduced the quality of life for the victims. Many victims changed their routines to avoid confrontation. Children were kept indoors or taken elsewhere to play. Adults left home early or returned late. In one case washing was hung out to dry after dark. In some cases the victims actually gave up their home and moved.

In conclusion, the impact of income inequalities leads many ethnic minorities to live and work in areas where they face emotional and physical abuse which has a detrimental effect on their wellbeing.

Racism in Rural Areas

In 2001 and 2005, *The Observer* published research it had undertaken using government statistics on racism in England and Wales. It found that ethnic minorities faced a proportionately greater risk from racism in rural areas, where ethnic minority concentrations were low, than in urban areas where there were high concentrations. Areas such as Devon and Cornwall, Northumbria, Cumbria and Durham, with small ethnic minority populations, had some of the biggest problems.

The safest areas were places such as Leicestershire and London where there were high concentrations of ethnic minorities. In these areas less than 1% of the population reported overt racism towards

Family members follow the coffin of murdered teenager Anthony Walker as it is carried from the Anglican Cathedral in Liverpool, following his funeral in August 2005. The 18-year-old student was bludgeoned with an axe in a park in Huyton, near Liverpool by two white males in a racially motivated attack. Prior to the attack the white men had shouted racist abuse at Anthony who had responded by walking away.

them, whereas in Northumbria 5% of minorities reported being victims of racism. One of the most rural counties in England, Cumbria, has the worst record for recorded racist crime in England.

POLICIES AND STRATEGIES TO DEAL WITH RACE INEQUALITIES IN WEALTH

Race Relations Act 1976

The *Race Relations Act* outlaws discrimination on the grounds of colour, race, nationality and ethnic origin. The law makes direct and indirect discrimination illegal. It makes racial discrimination unlawful in employment, training and related matters, in education, in the provision of goods, facilities and services, and in the disposal and management of properties.

The Act gives individuals a right of direct access to the civil courts and industrial tribunals for legal remedies for unlawful discrimination. These complaints or allegations are brought by the Commission for Racial Equality.

The Commission for Racial Equality (CRE) was created by the *Race Relations Act* to help enforce the legislation and to promote equality of opportunity and good relations between people of different racial groups. The Commission has the responsibility for advising the government on the working of the Act and it is also the principal source of information and advice for the general public about the Act. The Commission can assist individuals who believe they have been discriminated against.

In 2006, the government proposed replacing the CRE with a Commission for Equality and Human Rights (CEHR). The CEHR would also incorporate the existing commissions for gender and disability and have added responsibility for religion or belief, sexual orientation, age and human rights. The CRE opposed being included in the CEHR and after representations to the government its independence was guaranteed until 2009.

The CRE deals with enquiries from people who believe they are the victims of discrimination. In 2004, the CRE's legal staff dealt with a total of 5,443 enquiries. The vast majority only needed advice, but 567 needed significant professional services from CRE lawyers. Just over 50% of the applications for assistance which were considered in 2004 were related to employment, and almost 60% came from the public sector. The largest ethnic group to be given assistance was Black African, followed by Black Caribbean and Indian. Furthermore, twice as many men as women were assisted. The majority of cases were settled out of court and of those which went to court ten were settled for a total amount of £18,000.

A second important function of the CRE is to provide guidance to employers and service providers on how to prevent discrimination from happening. The CRE is in the process of redrafting its code to take account of the changes in UK and European law since its code first came into effect in 1984. The code aims to ensure race equality in the workplace.

The CRE also investigates organisations. In 2004, it reported on its formal investigation into the police service in England and Wales. The main finding was that, of the twenty police forces and authorities investigated, 90% did not have an adequate race equality scheme in place. By the end of 2004, every force had put in place appropriate schemes to meet the requirements of the CRE.

The CRE also had a significant input in the response to the government's *Strength in Diversity* consultation paper which aimed to develop a community cohesion and race equality strategy. It helped to shape the final document, *Improving Opportunity, Strengthening Society*, which was published in 2005. (See page 55.)

Every government department has to produce a Public Service Agreement (PSA) which sets out its objectives and performance targets over a three-year period. The CRE influenced the departments to include specific racial equality targets and monitoring to cover the following:

- increase the employment rate of ethnic minorities
- promote ethnic diversity in the labour market
- educational attainment
- access to higher education
- health inequalities
- confidence in the criminal justice system
- housing supply and housing conditions

The departments responsible for these targets are now publicly accountable for tackling racial inequalities in these areas as a contribution to the government-wide target to 'reduce race inequalities and build community cohesion'.

The Race Relations (Amendment) Act 2000

The 2000 Act extends the 1976 Act to cover public authorities. It also places a positive duty on certain listed public authorities to prevent discrimination occurring and to promote racial equality. It was introduced in response to advice from the CRE and in the light of the criticisms of the police service in the MacPherson Report. The 2000 Act aims to eliminate institutional discrimination in the UK.

The following are some of the main provisions of the Act.

❖ Direct and indirect discrimination is outlawed in public authority functions not previously covered by the 1976 Act.

❖ 'Public authority' is defined widely so that it includes private sector and voluntary organisations when they are carrying out public functions. This covers any organisation which has a contract to do work for a public body such as a local authority or the NHS or is in receipt of funding from such a body.

❖ A positive duty is placed on listed public authorities to promote racial equality.

❖ The liability of Chief Constables is extended to cover all activities of the police service. In the past it was only possible to sue individual police officers but now the Chief Constable is responsible for the actions of all officers. The Home Office has recommended that Chief Constables take reasonable steps to ensure that officers under their direction and control do not racially discriminate against anyone.

❖ Greater protection is provided against discrimination in public appointments.

It is now the duty of every public body to eliminate unlawful racial discrimination, to promote equality of opportunity between people of different racial groups, and to promote good relations between people of different racial groups. This includes education, health provision, local government and all departments of government.

The Crime and Disorder Act 1998

The government introduced this legislation to enable courts to recognise that there was a racial element to an offence and to increase the sentence as a consequence. The charge of racial aggravation can be added to an existing offence. If the judge accepts the prosecution's case that the defendant demonstrated racial hostility at the time of the offence or immediately before it, or that the offence was motivated wholly or partly by racial hostility, then the sentence can be increased by up to two years.

The Crime and Disorder Act 1998 (Amended)

Criminal Justice (Scotland) Act 2003

These Acts introduced Anti-Social Behaviour Orders (ASBOs) to both sides of the border. In Scotland the law requires local authorities or housing associations to apply to a court to issue an ASBO on unruly residents. ASBOs can be used to prohibit an individual from indulging in specific behaviour, including racist behaviour, and from entering a particular area. The following extract was taken from an ASBO granted by a court:

The defendant is prohibited from:

1 *Engaging in conduct which causes or is likely to cause harassment, alarm or distress to other residents of [x] and the surrounding area.*
2 *Using foul, offensive or racist language which is or is likely to be threatening, abusive or insulting to residents of or visitors to the said area.*
3 *Assaulting, threatening or intimidating residents of or visitors to the said area.*
4 *Threatening to cause, attempting to cause or causing criminal damage to property or premises within the said area.*

The Employment Equality (Religion or Belief) Regulations 2003

The regulations outlaw discrimination in employment and vocational training on the grounds of religion or belief. They extend the provisions of the *Race Relations Act* to employees to protect them from prejudice, discrimination and harassment in the workplace. The regulations make the following illegal:

● *Direct discrimination* – treating people less favourably than others on grounds of their religion or belief.
● *Indirect discrimination* – applying a provision, criterion or practice which disadvantages people of a particular religion or belief.

The police introduced a uniform turban instead of the standard issue hat to allow Sikhs to join the force.

● *Harassment* – unwanted conduct which violates people's dignity or creates an intimidating, hostile, degrading, humiliating or offensive environment.
● *Victimisation* – treating people less favourably because of something they have done under, or in connection with, the Regulations, e.g. made a formal complaint of discrimination or given evidence in a tribunal case.

The One Scotland Campaign

One Scotland is the Scottish Executive's campaign aimed at tackling racism. The aim is to make people aware of racist attitudes and behaviour and to demonstrate how these harm the victims and diminish the country. It aims to show the contribution that all cultures have made to Scottish society and make Scotland no place for racism.

The campaign has taken its message to the public in a variety of ways through advertising campaigns on the TV and by sponsoring events such as the *One Scotland St Andrews Day Ceilidh*, *Live and Loud 2005* and *Polaroid Mosaic*. *Polaroid Mosaic* took the message of the campaign the length and breadth of Scotland in shopping centres from Glasgow, Ayr and Galashiels in the south right up to the Isle of Skye and Stornoway in the north. It created a mosaic of the faces of the people of Scotland in the shape of the *One Scotland Many Cultures* logo. It is made up of over 1,100 individual Polaroid head and shoulder snapshots.

In sport it has included the 'Show racism the red card' campaign. It worked with the STUC to launch *The One Workplace Equal Rights* project to tackle racism and promote equal opportunities in workplaces across Scotland.

It provided funds for Heartstone, a voluntary organisation which uses stories and photographs to reach young people in schools, colleges and youth groups. The stories are used to stimulate discussion and debate, and provide the basis for practical project work which leads to changing attitudes and behaviour.

Through these and other activities the *One Scotland Campaign* aims to use education and involvement to persuade all Scots of the positive benefits of eliminating racism from Scottish society.

Other policies and strategies to deal with race inequalities in wealth
● New Deal
● Working Tax Credit
● Child Tax Credit
● National Minimum Wage
● Welfare Benefits
(See Chapter 5.)

IMPROVING LIFE CHANCES FOR ALL

This strategy signals the arrival of a comprehensive cross-government Public Service Agreement target to monitor and reduce race inequalities between 2005 and 2008. It includes specific goals to reduce perceptions of discrimination in a wide range of public services, reduce employment inequalities and monitor the progress of minority ethnic communities across major public services, from education to housing.

Measures in the strategy can be divided into the following categories:

In Education

The government will better target the £162 million Ethnic Minority Achievement Grant to help schools focus on those ethnic groups who are struggling to perform. It will also improve the teaching of English for pupils for whom it is a second language and increase the recruitment of minority ethnic teachers to at least 9% of those entering the profession during the next three years.

In the Labour Market

The government will provide more tailored support for jobseekers from disadvantaged groups. It also aims to improve literacy and numeracy among at least 1.5 million adults, particularly from disadvantaged groups.

In Health

Part of the strategy will include providing greater patient choice by tailoring services to meet the particular needs of different cultural and ethnic groups. Through its overall NHS programme to reduce all health inequalities the government will take particular action to tackle inequalities experienced by minority ethnic groups, such as the disproportionately high levels of heart disease among South Asians.

In Housing

Overcrowding and the number living in poor quality accommodation is greater, and resident satisfaction lower, among nearly all Black and minority ethnic communities. The government therefore aims to:

- ensure that all social tenants live in decent accommodation by 2010
- ensure that at least 70% of vulnerable owner-occupiers and private tenants are in decent accommodation through greater help with home improvements—particularly focusing on Black and minority ethnic communities
- continue to monitor and tackle discrimination through the work of the Audit Commission and the Commission for Racial Equality's forthcoming code of practice on housing.

In Policing and the Criminal Justice System

The government will introduce a new statutory duty on police authorities to promote diversity within their forces and ensure that assessment and selection panels are more representative of the Black and minority ethnic communities they serve. They will also provide better support and training for prison officers and those managing the Criminal Justice System locally to help them address discrimination.

Legislation

In 2003, the government introduced protection from discrimination in employment and vocational training on the grounds of religion or belief. It now plans to go further by introducing legislation against discrimination in the provision of goods, facilities and services on the grounds of religion or belief.

The establishment of the new Commission for Equality and Human Rights will, by 2009, help provide a more integrated approach to promoting overall equality and good relations between communities.

Building Community Cohesion

The strategy sets out to promote a sense of belonging and cohesion amongst all groups, setting out a vision for a British society in which:

- young people from different communities grow up with a sense of common belonging
- new immigrants are integrated
- people have opportunities to develop a greater understanding of the range of cultures that contribute to our strength as a country
- people from all backgrounds have opportunities to participate in civic society
- racism is unacceptable
- extremists who promote hatred are marginalised.

Delivering the strategy

In delivering this strategy the government will seek to work with businesses, community groups, and individuals. Business has a vital role to play in ensuring that the talent of all is used, while community groups will be essential to progress in strengthening the sense of belonging and cohesion in society. Individuals have a responsibility themselves to contribute to society and use services appropriately.

Source: http://www.crimereduction.gov.uk/racial13.htm

Chapter 5

Measures to deal with inequalities in wealth

A Labour government was elected in 1997 with a social policy which promoted social inclusion. It wanted to reconnect those who were poor and who had become disconnected from work, education, health and the community. The emphasis was to get those who were unemployed, but able to work, off benefit dependency and into work.

The government created pathways to make it easier for the unemployed to retrain, develop skills and find employment. At the same time it made participation compulsory by denying benefits to those who sought to avoid the opportunities on offer.

It also made work financially more attractive. Welfare was targeted at tax credits for those in work while the level of benefits paid to the unemployed, such as Jobseeker's Allowance (JSA), were allowed to fall to make them relatively less attractive. The value of benefits has declined by 20% relative to average income since the mid-1990s. Particular benefits for the unemployed also had time limits imposed so that an unemployed person had to accept training or a job and could not continue on JSA indefinitely.

The government aimed to reduce the levels of child poverty in the UK. It increased support for families with dependent children. Tax credits and initiatives such as Sure Start were introduced to help raise children out of poverty.

Consecutive Labour governments put in place a variety of measures to carry forward their social inclusion policies.

Labour government measures to increase the level of employment:

✔ Jobcentre Plus
✔ New Deals for
  ● young people
  ● the long-term unemployed
  ● lone parents
  ● disabled people
✔ National Minimum Wage
✔ Working Tax Credit
✔ Child Tax Credit

Additional help for younger people seeking employment was introduced in the form of Skillseekers and Modern Apprenticeships.

The Labour government also introduced measures to provide income for those not employed. These measures were

❖ Jobseeker's Allowance
❖ Income Support changes targeted at children (replaced and enhanced by Child Tax Credit and Working Tax Credit)
❖ State pension
❖ Pension Credit (replaced and enhanced Minimum Income Guarantee for Pensioners)
❖ Winter Fuel Payments
❖ Changes to income tax and National Insurance Contributions

JOBCENTRE PLUS

Jobcentre Plus is run by the Department for Work and Pensions. The Jobcentre Plus network is made up of Jobcentre Plus offices, Jobcentres and Social Security offices. There is a Jobcentre Plus office in all large towns and cities.

Jobcentre Plus provides a wide range of services designed to help a person find employment and claim the correct benefits when unemployed. Each individual is given a personal adviser to help them negotiate their path back into employment. Some services provided are

◆ Jobseeker Direct which is a phone service supplying information about vacancies in the local area and beyond. If someone is interested in a job, Jobcentre Plus can tell them how to apply, help them to send an application form, and phone to arrange an interview.

◆ The Jobcentre Plus website provides on-line job searches. The site has nationwide lists of vacancies and application forms. It has information to help people to create CVs, and advice on writing letters of application and other aspects of finding employment.

◆ Jobpoints are found in all offices. These touch-screen kiosks allow people to search for all available jobs. Jobpoints are also to be located in supermarkets and in other places in the community.

◆ The EURES network allows people to search for jobs throughout the EU.

◆ Programme Centres provide a range of help, support and advice on both searching for a job and getting training. They offer practical help such as developing a CV, preparing for an interview and getting free stamps, newspapers and stationery. They also run local courses.

◆ Better Off Calculation is for people who are thinking of starting work or who have been offered a job. A personal adviser will calcu-

late the effect on a person's income of coming off benefits and going into a particular job.

◆ Work Trial allows someone to try out a job vacancy for up to fifteen working days. This is a voluntary programme and it is up to the individual to prove her/his ability to do the job. Benefits are not affected if the person leaves or turns down a firm offer of a job.

◆ Learndirect provides opportunities for someone to gain knowledge and skills which would improve their chances of getting a job. The participant chooses what to learn, when to learn and the pace of learning.

◆ WorkPath programmes are designed to help disabled people

who want to find jobs or stay in work. Each programme is designed to help the disabled overcome or remove the barriers they face in finding employment. The three WorkPath programmes are

• Access to Work,
• Work Preparation and
• WORKSTEP.

WORKSTEP provides tailored support for disabled people who have more complicated barriers to getting and keeping a job. This is long-term support for both employer and employee in order to maintain employment.

◆ Jobcentre Plus also provides practical support and financial advice about benefits, tax credits and childcare.

57

THE NEW DEAL

The New Deal was introduced to give unemployed people help in getting back into employment or through training provide them with the new skills necessary for them to get work. When someone joins the New Deal they are given a personal adviser. The personal adviser remains their contact person throughout the programme. Having discussed the options and having taken time to understand the individual's needs, the personal adviser helps plan a route into employment which may include:

■ work experience with an employer or voluntary organisation

■ training for a particular job

■ a course to create the skills that employers want

■ help with job applications

■ practice in interview techniques

Personal advisers also have many local contacts in the workplace and will continue to assist individuals to find a job if they remain unemployed after the period of training.

The New Deal consists of seven different schemes aimed at different groups of unemployed people.

Putting yourself in the picture with New Deal 50 plus

new deal★

▲ *The New Deal for Young People* is a compulsory scheme for people aged between 18 and 24 who have claimed Jobseeker's Allowance continuously for six months or more. In some cases individuals are invited to join the programme earlier.

▲ *The New Deal 25 plus* is also a compulsory scheme and is for people over 25 who have continuously claimed Jobseeker's Allowance for eighteen months. Again individuals may be invited to join earlier.

▲ *The New Deal 50 plus* is a voluntary scheme aimed at helping older people to find employment. Any person over 50 who has been receiving one or more of a list of benefits such as Income Support, Jobseeker's Allowance, Incapacity Benefit or Pension Credit for six months or more can apply.

▲ *The New Deal for Lone Parents* is voluntary. Although lone parents are offered New Deal interviews, participation is not compulsory. Anyone bringing up children as a lone parent whose youngest child is under 16 years old and who is either not working, or is working less than sixteen hours per week can join. The personal adviser offers advice and help about finding childcare as well as offering training. Information is also provided about how benefits will be affected when a person starts work and about any tax credit entitlement. Although this is a voluntary programme, since 2002 it has been compulsory for lone parents to attend regular 'work-focused' interviews.

▲ *The New Deal for Disabled People* is a voluntary scheme. It is provided through a network of Job Brokers who are chosen for their experience in working with people with health conditions or disabilities.

▲ *The New Deal for Partners* is voluntary and is aimed at helping the partners of long-term jobless people to find work.

TAX AND BENEFIT SYSTEM CHANGES

The government altered the tax and benefits system to increase the difference in income between those who were in work and those who were not. The intention was to create an incentive for those who were unemployed to get back into work. To further increase the differential it introduced the National Minimum Wage to raise the basic level of income for those in low paid employment.

▲ *The New Deal for Musicians* aims to help unemployed, aspiring musicians into a sustainable career in the music industry. It covers all types of music and even includes DJs. It provides open learning materials on a wide variety of aspects of the industry including performing, recording and production, marketing, and teaching music. The New Deal for Musicians is also part of the New Deal for Young People and the New Deal 25 plus.

The National Minimum Wage

In April 1999 the Labour government introduced a National Minimum Wage (NMW) to set hourly rates below which wages are not allowed to fall. The NMW applies to nearly every worker in the UK and the rates set are based on the recommendations of the Low Pay Commission. There are different rates for workers of different ages.

In 2006, the NMW rates were

- for an adult (22 and over) – £5.35 per hour (£214.00 before tax for a 40 hour week).

- for someone aged 18 to 21 – £4.45 per hour (£178.00 before tax for a 40 hour week).

- for people aged 16 - 17 - £3.30 per hour (£132.00 before tax for a 40 hour week). However, 16– and 17- year old apprentices are exempt from this rate.

The government's aim with the NMW is to encourage more workers to find jobs because wage levels are higher and there is a greater gap in income compared with those remaining on benefit. The Low Pay Commission estimates that approximately 1.9 million adults and 170,000 youths got an increase in their wages as a result of the NMW uprating in 2006. That is about 8% of the workforce. These workers are mainly in hospitality, catering and cleaning, retail, hairdressing, agriculture, security, social care and textile and footwear manufacture.

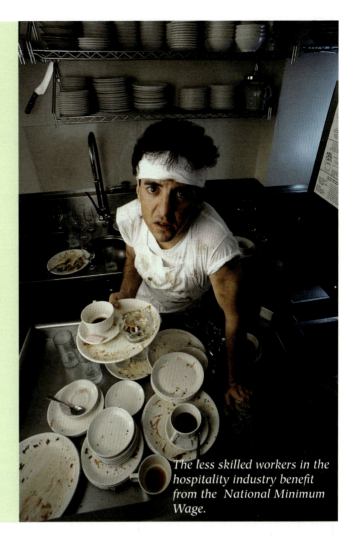

The less skilled workers in the hospitality industry benefit from the National Minimum Wage.

Working Tax Credit

Tax credits are at the heart of the Labour government's welfare policy. Since 1997, the Chancellor has created a social security system in which the tax and benefits systems are integrated. The emphasis of support has shifted from handouts to tax credits in order to make work financially more attractive.

Working Tax Credit (WTC) is a tax adjustment. The government calculates how much money a person is entitled to and gives this figure to the employer who reduces the amount of tax taken from their wages. WTC allows low paid workers to retain more of their wages by reducing the amount taken in tax and thereby increasing their take-home pay. By increasing the differential in income between those in work and those living on benefits, the combination of WTC and NMW has significantly reduced the benefit trap which has been a major barrier preventing many moving away from benefits and into work.

WTC has a childcare element. Where either a lone parent, or both partners work for at least sixteen hours a week, they are entitled to up to 70% of eligible childcare costs. They can get assistance of up to £300 a week for a family with two or more children, or £175 a week for a single child.

Child Tax Credit

Child Tax Credit (CTC) is paid by the government directly to families with children. They may be employed or unemployed and may have a combined income of up to £58,175. There are two parts to CTC—a family element and a child element. In tax year 2006 – 2007 the family element was worth £545 per year (£1090 with the first year baby element). The child element is £1,765 per child per year.

All families who have combined incomes of less than £58,175 a year will get at least £545 a year from the 'family element' of the credit. In addition, families with incomes of up to £13,910 a year should qualify for the 'child element' of £1,765 a year for each child.

Although Child Tax Credit makes no distinction between those in work and those not in work, it provides a guarantee of income for those who are moving from benefits into work.

Skillseekers

All 16, 17, and 18-year-olds are eligible to join Skillseekers. It is run in Scotland by Local Enterprise Companies (LECs). It is a training programme in which young people can work towards a recognised qualification in the workplace with day release to study at college. Employers are encouraged to take part in the scheme because they get help with the costs of training.

All young people on the Skillseekers programme are working to gain either Scottish or National Vocational Qualifications which are available for nearly every kind of job. Each vocational qualification is made up of units covering different aspects of a particular job. Participants can work at a pace that suits them and their employer.

Careers Scotland Centres can help young people who do not have a job to find a placement through work experience or they can place them with an LEC which will find employment for them and organise training.

Modern Apprenticeships

The Modern Apprentice programme is similar to Skillseekers but is for people aiming to get intermediate level vocational qualifications (SVQ Level 3 or above). Furthermore, people of any age can apply. Modern Apprenticeships offer people aged 16 and over the chance of paid employment linked to training at craft, technician or management level. Modern Apprentices gain expertise and knowledge through on-the-job training and assessment. Many also attend college to gain the theory relating to the occupation they have chosen.

Although these apprenticeships are mainly for people looking to gain Level 3 vocational qualifications, there are opportunities in some to start at Level 2 and in others to progress to Level 4. Each course has a core skills element which includes communication, working with others, numeracy, information technology and problem solving. In 2006, there were over 32,000 Modern Apprentices at some stage of training in Scotland. The seven most popular 'frameworks' in Scotland are Construction, Customer Services, Business Administration, Motor Vehicles, Engineering, Electro-technical and Hospitality.

Most employers who have been involved in the Modern Appren-

ticeship scheme agree that it has benefited their company. It helps both to create a better trained workforce with recognised qualifications and to retain staff. Employers also report that participants take Modern Apprenticeship training more seriously than other types of training.

Jobseeker's Allowance

To be able to claim Jobseeker's Allowance (JSA) a person must be able to work, be available for work and be actively seeking work. Someone must be on a New Deal Scheme in order to satisfy these conditions. A person will be expected to find a job or move into training. If not, JSA will be stopped. Any person not available for work, such as a lone parent, a full-time carer or someone who is long-term sick, cannot claim JSA.

There are two types of JSA. One is Contribution-based JSA and the other is Income-based JSA. Contribution-based JSA is for those who have paid sufficient National Insurance Contributions in the preceding period. It is paid at a fixed rate for up to twenty six weeks.

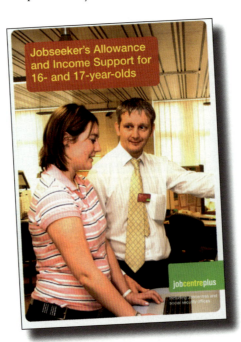

Jobseeker's Allowance and Income Support for 16- and 17-year-olds

Income-based JSA is a means-tested benefit for those who do not qualify for Contribution-based JSA by not having sufficient National Insurance Contributions. Any person with savings over £16,000

does not qualify and having savings over £6,000 reduces the amount of income-based JSA a person can get. JSA is not normally available for people aged 16 or 17. This group usually need to claim Income Support.

Income Support

Income Support (IS) is for people on a low income between the ages of 16 and 59 who cannot work. The people covered by IS are those who are not able to work because of illness or disability, people who care for a sick or disabled person and lone parents who are responsible for at least one child under 16.

IS is a means-tested benefit and the amount an individual receives depends on their age, the size of their family, any disability they or members of their family have, whether the person is caring for someone, whether they have savings over £6,000 (including partner's savings), and any earnings by the claimant and their partner. People can apply for IS to make up the difference between the income they receive from other benefits and the IS level they are entitled to.

People cannot claim IS if they work for more than sixteen hours per week or if their spouse or partner works for more than twenty four hours per week. Students are also excluded.

A person who is entitled to Income Support automatically qualifies for free dental care, free prescriptions, free school meals, Housing Benefit and Council Tax Benefit. The rules that regulate IS are complex and it is difficult to calculate the level of income a person is entitled to claim. As a result many people do not claim all the Income Support that is due to them.

In 2005, 2.1 million people were receiving IS. The disabled accounted for 53% of the total and lone parents were 37%. 80% of claimants had been on IS for more than one year and 42% had claimed it for more than five years (See Table 5.1.) Income Support levels are

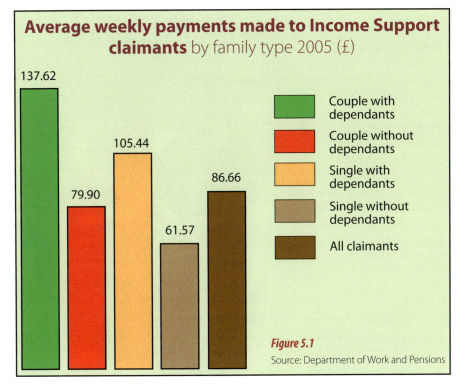

Average weekly payments made to Income Support claimants by family type 2005 (£)

- 137.62 — Couple with dependants
- 79.90 — Couple without dependants
- 105.44 — Single with dependants
- 61.57 — Single without dependants
- 86.66 — All claimants

Figure 5.1
Source: Department of Work and Pensions

very low. A single person without dependants on National Minimum Wage before any tax and credit entitlement will earn over £200 per week. This is over three times more than the same person on Income Support. (See Figure 5.1.)

Average duration of IS claims, 2005	
Under 1 year	18.8%
1 year up to 5 years	38.8%
5 years or more	42.4%

Table 5.1
Source: Department of Work and Pensions

Other Benefits for those on low incomes paid by national government:
- Prescription charges
- Free eye tests (available to all in Scotland from April 2006)
- Dental Treatment

Benefits paid through Local Authorities:
- Housing Benefit
- Council Tax Benefit
- Free School Meals
- Clothing Vouchers

BASIC STATE PENSION

The cornerstone of the government's welfare insurance for the elderly is the basic state pension. It is based on the number of years a person has either paid or has been credited with National Insurance Contributions (NICs). Currently it is paid to men who have reached 65 or women who have reached 60. However, between 2010 and 2020 women's age for qualifying will rise to 65.

To receive the full basic state pension a person must have made contributions for at least 90% of their working years calculated from their sixteenth birthday. If someone has not paid enough NICs because they have been looking after children or caring for someone long-term, the number of qualifying years will be reduced. This is known as 'Home Responsibilities Protection'.

Anyone who does not qualify for the full basic state pension, but who has 25% or more of the qualifying years, will get a proportionate weekly basic state pension. Anyone with less than 25% is not entitled to this pension. However, if they are over 80 they can get a 'non-contributory' or 'over-80 pension' which was £50.50 a week for 2006 – 2007.

The basic state pension is personal and cannot be passed on to someone else when a person dies.

The basic state pension is uprated annually. In 1974 the link between state pensions and earnings ensured that state pensions kept up with the rate at which salaries were rising. However, in 1980 Margaret Thatcher replaced that link with a link to prices. With earnings rising faster than prices, pensioners' incomes have fallen behind the incomes of those in work.

The Turner Report

Addressing pensioner poverty in the future has become a major concern for the government. As pensioners live longer and the birth rate falls, the burden of funding increasing pension demands will fall on a decreasing working population pushing taxation ever higher. In 2005, 21% of the population were past retirement age, a figure which will rise to 30% by 2050.

The Turner Report advised increasing the state pension age for both men and women from 65 to 68 by 2050. In return, the commission said, the basic state pension should in future rise in line with earnings, rather than inflation. The Report also proposed that all employees should join a new National Pension Savings Scheme (NPSS) if they are not in a company pension scheme. People would have the right to opt out of NPSS. The contributions to NPSS will be invested as shares, bonds and property, while the ordinary state pension would continue to be paid for out of tax and National Insurance Contributions.

The future, according to the Turner Report, involves people having a longer working life, a later age for retiral, saving more for themselves and receiving higher pensions once they have retired. Following the Report's publication, the leadership of the Labour Party agreed to restore the link between pensions and earnings in 2012 in return for the retirement age for both men and women rising to 68 by 2050.

Pension Credit

Pension Credit guarantees a minimum income for everyone of pensionable age. In 2006, pension credit for a single pensioner was £114.05 and for a pensioner couple it was £174.05.

A person over 60 and single will get the difference between £114.05 and their total weekly income if it is less than this. A couple will get the difference between £174.05 and their joint total weekly income if it is less than this—even if one is under 60. A single pensioner with a state pension of £74.05 will get Pension Credit of £40.00 (£114.05 minus £74.05). Anyone who has additional needs, such as caring for a dependant, or who is severely disabled or who has particular housing costs may be entitled to more. Pension Credit is paid weekly into the pensioner's account in their bank, building society or Post Office as one amount along with their basic state pension. Everyone aged over 75 gets a free TV licence.

Winter Fuel Payments

Each year pensioners receive a one-off payment to help them pay their home heating bills through the winter. The amount they receive varies according to their age and whether they receive Pension Credit or not. In 2006 – 07, the payment for those aged 60 to 79 was £200 for a single person or £300 if a couple qualified. For someone over 80, the payment was £300 or up to £450 if they were part of a couple.

Free Personal Care for the Elderly

The Scottish Parliament voted to provide free personal care for the elderly rather than have it means-tested as in England. It provides payments of up to £145 per week plus £65 of nursing costs for elderly people at home, in hospital or in care homes. It is for people who need help with washing, bathing, shaving, using the toilet, dressing, bed changing, simple medication, and diet and eating.

Sure Start

Sure Start is a programme that combines health, social services and early education provision to tackle child poverty and social exclusion. Through working with parents and children it tries to improve the physical, intellectual and social development of babies and young children to promote their physical and intellectual well-being at home and school.

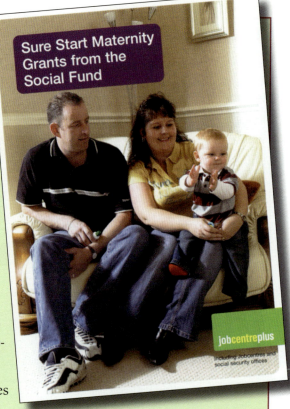

Sure Start Maternity Grants from the Social Fund

jobcentreplus
including Jobcentres and social security offices

Across the UK there are 524 local programmes helping up to 400,000 children in disadvantaged areas. In Scotland all local authorities have been given Sure Start funding which will be £60 million in 2008. Sure Start funding is highly focused on the most disadvantaged areas, including rural areas which have specific problems.

Sure Start Children's Centres in the most disadvantaged areas offer:

- good quality early learning led by specialist teachers
- full day care provision for children (minimum ten hours a day, five days a week, forty eight weeks a year)
- child and family health services, including ante-natal services
- family support services including outreach support
- a childminder network
- effective links with Jobcentre Plus to support parents/carers who wish to consider training or employment

There is less intense provision in areas which are not so disadvantaged.

The policy was introduced in 2002, and by 2005 there were 40,000 people receiving care at home and a further 9,000 in care homes. By 2006, the Scottish Executive provided £162 million annually to local councils whose social work departments are required to provide and administer the system. However, the thirty two Scottish councils claimed this was £70 million short of the annual cost of provision and some councils were accused of finding ways of charging or of creating waiting lists to slow down the provision to save cash.

A review report by the Scottish Parliament Health Committee in 2006 said that the policy had been a great success by bringing "greater security and dignity to elderly people". The Committee called on the Parliament to change the law to prevent councils from creating waiting lists and to introduce time limits for assessments. It demanded that the service be centrally funded and that all existing claims be backdated.

EFFECTIVENESS OF GOVERNMENT POLICIES

Reducing Unemployment

The New Deal, National Minimum Wage and Working Tax Credits, combined with improvements in the economy, encouraged many more people into employment. The UK unemployment rate fell from nearly 7% in 1997 to 5% in 2001 and remained around that level up to 2006. Employment rates have risen over the same period. In 1997, 77.7% of men and 67.4% of women were working. By 2005, these figures had increased to 79.0% and 70.1% respectively.

The various New Deal Programmes have been successful at getting people back into work. The New Deal for Young People has reduced the level of long-term unemployment among young people. In Scotland, of those leaving the New Deal to go into work, 78% went into sustained jobs. The figure for the New Deal for Adults was 77%.

Reducing Low Pay

The National Minimum Wage has helped to tackle the problem of low pay in the UK. It has raised the pay of about 1.3 million people or 5% of the workforce. About three-quarters of those who have benefited are women. Before the NMW was introduced, 6% of jobs were below the level of the minimum wage. Within one year of its introduction, the NMW had reduced this figure to 2%. In 2006, around 1% of jobs in the UK were estimated to be paying rates below the NMW level.

Compared to international rates the level set for the NMW in the UK is low. In the UK the NMW is 40% of mean hourly pay rates. It is higher than the USA (32%) and four other industrial countries, but lags behind several others such as France (50%), Australia and Holland both of which have minimum wage rates set at over 60% of mean earnings. When it was introduced in 1999, the NMW was only 36% of the mean hourly wage so over time it is gradually increasing.

Reducing Poverty

Table 5.2 shows that poverty grew significantly from 1979, peaking in 2000. Since the Labour Party was elected in 1997, government policy has directed greater help towards moving children and pensioners out of poverty. Poverty is falling in households where there are children or pensioners. (See Table 5.3.) Between 1997 and 2003, there were 700,000 fewer children and 500,000 fewer pensioners living in low income households.

People living in poverty in the UK

	Number (million)	Percent
1979	5.0	9
1996	14.1	24
2000	15.5	25
2003	12.4	23

Table 5.2 Source: ONS

Who are the Poor in Scotland?

	Average 94/97	Average 00/03
Pensioners	21%	17%
Children	30%	27%
Working age adults with children	23%	20%
Working age adults with no children	26%	36%

Table 5.3 Source: Households below average income, DWP

Table 5.4 shows that recent government measures have had mixed success in dealing with poverty in the UK. They have reduced the numbers on low incomes and increased the level of employment. On balance, the government policy of welfare to work has managed to get more people into employment and its aim of reducing childhood and pensioner poverty has had an impact.

Indicator Trends for the UK over the last 5 years or so

Income	
Numbers in low income	Improved
Low income by age group	Mixed
Low income by family type	Improved
Low income by work status	na
Out-of-work benefit levels	Mixed

Children	
In low income households	Improved
In workless households	Improved
Concentration of poor children	Steady
Low birth weight babies	Worsened
Child health and well-being	Steady
Underage pregnancies	Steady
Low attainment at school (11-year-olds)	Improved
Low attainment at school (16-year-olds)	Steady

Young adults	
Without a basic qualification	Steady
In low income households	Steady
Unemployment	Steady

Low pay	
Working-age adults aged 25+	Steady
Low income and work	Worsened
Low income and disability	Steady
Wanting paid work	Improved
Work and disability	Improved
Workless households	Steady
Low pay by gender	Steady
Insecure at work	Steady

Pensioners	
In low income households	Improved
No private income	Improved
Non-take-up of benefits	Worsened
Excess winter deaths	Steady
Limiting longstanding illness	Steady
Help to live at home	Worsened

Table 5.4

Source: Extract from *Monitoring poverty and social exclusion in the UK 2005* Joseph Rowntree Foundation

Relative poverty has fallen in the last few years due to improvements in employment rates and in the levels of some benefits, as well as the introduction of tax credits.

Reducing Child Poverty

Measures taken between 1997 and 2003 – 4 have resulted in 1.3 million fewer children across the UK living in poverty. In Scotland, the proportion of children living in income poverty has fallen from 30% to 27% in recent years.

Changes to the child tax and benefits package since 1999 have lifted large numbers of families with children out of poverty. The government is on target to achieve its aim of reducing the number of children in relative poverty if it continues to make the same level of progress in the future.

Helping Lone Parents

Lone parents have benefited from the introduction of tax credits and there is a high level of uptake. 40% of lone working mothers avoid poverty because of tax credits. Only 8% of low paid lone working mothers live in household poverty.

Income from full-time paid work is the most important way for lone parents to escape poverty. However, the high cost of childcare can be a barrier to taking up paid work and can make people worse off in work than if they remain on benefits. Therefore the provision of affordable, accessible and good quality childcare is essential if more lone parents are to find a way out of poverty.

Reducing Pensioner Poverty

In Scotland, pensioner poverty has fallen from 28% of pensioners in the mid-1990s to 20% in the mid-2000s. In the UK, pensioner poverty has fallen by 500,000 since 1999. Pensioners are now no more likely to be living in income poverty than non-pensioners.

The government has substantially increased the levels of means-tested benefits for pensioners, and it has

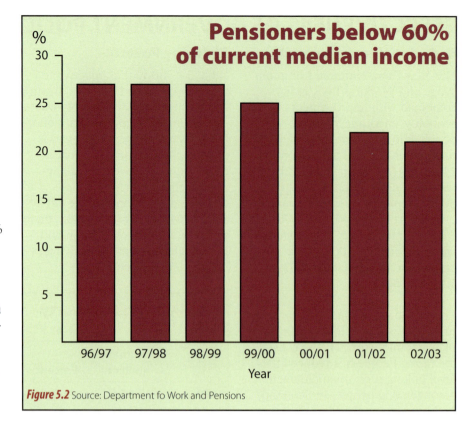

Figure 5.2 Source: Department fo Work and Pensions

introduced Pension Credit. However, a significant proportion do not claim these benefits. About a third of the pensioners in income poverty are entitled to Pension Credit but are not claiming it. Between a quarter and a third of pensioners entitled to claim the Minimum Income Guarantee, which was replaced by Pension Credit in October 2003, did not claim it. 33% of pensioners do not claim Council Tax Benefit and 10% of those entitled to Housing Benefit do not claim. One pensioner in three does not claim Income Support.

The system is complex and many do not claim through pride, ignorance or fear. The government will have to address the complexity of the system to improve benefit take-up in order to assist more pensioners out of poverty.

The UK has a higher number of avoidable winter deaths than comparable European countries such as Finland and Germany which experience more severe winters. Over the five winters from 2000 to 2004, between 20,000 and 50,000 people aged 65 and over were victims of avoidable winter deaths. Pensioners die from the cold or from ill health related to living in

cold, damp conditions. Children facing fuel poverty can suffer from educational under-achievement, social exclusion and ill health.

Fuel poverty is an issue the government has tried to address. In Scotland the Executive spent £250 million tackling fuel poverty and the number of fuel poor homes has fallen from 35% to around 13%. The Executive has funded the installation of central heating systems for 65,000 homes and more than 224,000 houses have been insulated under the Warm Deal scheme. Between 2002 and 2004 the number of homes classed as having 'good' energy efficiency rose from 30% to 40%. However, the majority continue to be classed as failing to meet minimum standards.

The government has tried to meet the problem of fuel poverty with Winter Fuel Payments but it has yet to solve the problem. The Fuel Poverty Advisory Group reported that a 10% rise in fuel prices pushes 400,000 consumers back into fuel poverty. In 2005 – 06 gas and electricity prices rose by 20%. The government's target of eradicating fuel poverty by 2016 will face increasing difficulties as energy prices continue to rise.

Chapter 6

Founding principles and structure of the NHS

In 1997 Labour came to power pledging to save the overstretched National Health Service and to restore "its founding principles". Before examining Labour's attempt to reduce health inequalities, it is important to examine the founding principles of the NHS and the development of the NHS since its inception. Chapter ten will consider the extent to which these principles are still being met today and will provide an overall assessment of health provision in Scotland and the United Kingdom.

THE BEVERIDGE REPORT

When the Beveridge Report was published in 1942, its recommendations amounted to a comprehensive attack on what Beveridge called 'the five giants' standing in the way of social progress, namely Want, Disease, Ignorance, Squalor and Idleness. The Report only dealt in detail with the first of these 'giants', Want—what we would now call poverty. Beveridge argued, however, that if people were to be kept out of poverty it would also be necessary for the other four 'giants' to be tackled.

A new national health system would make the population healthier, which would improve the productive resources of the country and reduce the costs of Social Security. Moreover, Beveridge expected that the costs to the state of providing this health care would, through time, decline, or at least remain stable, as the backlog of those suffering from ill health was eliminated.

Beveridge's 5 Giants

ELIMINATING *DISEASE*.......... by the creation of a new national health service

ELIMINATING *IGNORANCE* .... by the introduction of educational reforms

ELIMINATING *SQUALOR*........ by a programme to improve living conditions, in particular to provide adequate housing

ELIMINATING *IDLENESS* .... by the promotion of economic policies which would ensure high and stable levels of employment

ELIMINATING *WANT* .... by reforming and extending the social security system

The publication of the Beveridge Report was met with widespread public interest and enthusiasm. It quickly came to symbolise the hope that post-war British society could become more just and democratic.

Aneurin Bevan, the Labour Minister of Health, bought off the hospital consultants and specialists. By agreeing to their demands for private practice and merit awards he had, in his own words, "stuffed their mouths with gold". Although

they gained less from the discussions, the GPs were given the rights to be paid by a system of capitation fees and of having a semi-independent status.

THE FOUNDING PRINCIPLES OF THE NHS

The NHS came into operation on 5 July 1948, and in many ways represented a radical new commitment by the state. With the nationalisation of the hospitals, for example, a completely new element was included in the service. Aneurin Bevan's greatest achievement, however, was the creation of a national health system which was based on the principles of collective responsibility by the state for a genuinely universal and comprehensive range of services with equal access for all citizens.

Collectivist

The central aim of the *NHS Act* was that the state would accept the responsibility for providing a centrally organised health care system through collective action. The attitude of the BMA on behalf of the medical profession was, for a long time, hostile to state interference in what they called "the doctor-patient relationship".

The concept of collectivism guided by the principles of pooling and sharing, which had come to be identified with a nation fighting for its life during the Second World War, were now to become the aims of British domestic policy in general, and the new NHS in particular.

Central government became responsible for both the financial aspects and the direction of policy with regard to the health services. The Ministry of Health, later to become the Department of Health and Social Security, was responsible for the whole of the NHS in England and Wales, while the Secretary of State for Scotland had responsibility north of the border through the Scottish Home and Health Department.

Universal

Another aim of the new NHS was to provide for the whole population a range of health services which were free at the point of use. The previous insurance-based health system meant that access to personal health services without direct payment was limited to those who were covered under the terms of the 1911 *National Insurance Act*—less than half of the population. Instead, it was agreed that

this system should be replaced by one which included the principle of being universal. This would ensure that "the availability of necessary medical services shall not depend on whether people can afford to pay for them," and that "money should not be allowed to stand in the way of providing advice, early diagnosis and speedy treatment". The revenue of the new NHS was to come, not from an insurance-based system of finance, but predominantly from general taxation.

Comprehensive

The creation of the NHS also meant a commitment to provide "a comprehensive health service for the improvement of the physical and mental health of the people ... for the prevention, diagnosis and treatment of illness". The NHS was to be responsible for almost all aspects of the population's health care. Everyone, however, continued to have the right to obtain health care outside the service, if they so wished.

Equality

Finally, the *NHS Act* expressed commitment to eradicate inequalities in the provision of health care. Prior to the setting up of the NHS, the way the health services had developed meant that there was, in the words of Bevan, "a better service in the richer areas, a worse service in the poorer". Now, though, there was an opportunity "to achieve as nearly as possible a uniform standard of service for all—only with a national uniform standard of service can the state ensure that an equally good service is available everywhere".

The intention, then, was that both the quality and the quantity of the health care services available to individuals—the type of treatment, the number of GPs and specialist and consultant posts per head of population, the length of time a person had to wait in order to get treatment and the condition of hospitals—should be the same no matter in which part of the

country they happened to live. A unitary service, however, did not materialise.

FINANCE

Expenditure

In his Report, Beveridge had estimated that a national health service for Great Britain would cost about £170 million in its first year. Moreover, he had assumed that there was a fixed quantity of illness in the community and that this "pool of illness" would quickly reduce as the new improved system of medical care produced a healthier population. As a result, Beveridge believed that the cost of developing the service would be offset by this fall in demand, and so this £170 million, or its equivalent allowing for inflation, would still be enough twenty years later. The truth of the matter, however, was to prove to be quite different. By 1952–53 the expenditure on the health service had risen to £383 million, which was more than double Beveridge's original estimate. At the time, it appeared that NHS expenditure was out of control.

With the benefit of hindsight, however, it is difficult to see why the founders of the NHS had not foreseen this situation. The problem was that they had made the assumption that the cost of the NHS could be calculated by looking at the level of pre-war health care expenditure, and simply projecting this figure for the post-NHS period. For a number of reasons this method of calculation was to prove to be unsatisfactory.

☛ Prior to the setting up of the NHS, most people had had to choose between buying health care or spending their money in other ways, and there is little doubt that charges for medical services often deterred people, particularly those with low incomes, from seeking help. After 1948, of course, charges were abolished and so this element of choice no longer existed. The demand for this new universal health care system, free at the point of access, was far greater than the policy makers had expected.

☞ As we have seen, a basic underlying principle of the new system was that "the availability of necessary medical services shall not depend on whether people can afford to pay for them". This commitment was double-edged. Not only did it mean that patients were to get access to the health services without payment, but also that members of the medical profession were to be freed from all financial considerations when advising, diagnosing and treating their patients.

☞ The expansion and development of surgery, including new techniques in medicine, inevitably meant that there were many more treatable cases than before. More patients reached old age, which in turn meant that the health service had to cope with the more difficult problems of degenerative and chronic illness. Also, rising public expectations about the contribution medicine can make to us leading longer and healthier lives has meant that demand on the NHS is always likely to be limitless and, no matter how hard it tries, it will never be able to do enough.

Income

Not only did the policy makers miscalculate the expenditure of the NHS, they also failed to anticipate the implications of the system which was chosen to finance it. An insurance-based system was rejected and, instead, it was agreed that

the major proportion of the NHS's income was to come from general taxation. Approximately 88.3% of the National Health Service bill in 1950–51 came from this source, and the figure has fluctuated little since then. One consequence of this decision, however, has been that the NHS has had to compete with other government departments for money allocated to the public expenditure budget.

One way out of this dilemma was for the NHS to find additional means of funding, independent of the Treasury. In the 1950s, charges for dental work, spectacles and prescriptions were introduced. In effect, these decisions breached the original commitment of the NHS to provide a free service for all. Although charges have never contributed more than about 5% to the NHS budget, proposals to find alternative methods of financing the service have persistently reappeared on the agenda.

CONSERVATIVE HEALTH POLICIES

Before looking at the structure of the NHS today, a brief examination of the Conservatives' health reforms, referred to as the 'internal market', is required.

The Internal Market

The *NHS and Community Care Act 1990* introduced radical changes to the NHS. It created an internal market for health care based on a system of contracts for services between purchasers and providers.

Fundamental to this so-called internal market was the idea that money would follow patients. The assumption was that the internal market would make the service so efficient that financial crises would become a thing of the past. It would also help to increase consumer choice. Under the reforms, Health Boards (in Scotland) and Authorities (in England), Fundholding GPs, and private insurance companies became the buyers, purchasing care for their patients. The hospitals, whether trusts, directly managed, or from the private sector, became the sellers, competing with each other to provide the various services for patients. (See Figure 6.1.)

GP practices were encouraged to become fundholding practices which would enable GPs to take control of their own budgets. NHS Trusts were set up, which gave hospitals greater control over both their budgets and the decision making process. (See page 68.)

Fundholding GPs

Fundholding GPs could:
● use any money they saved from their budget to improve services within their practice
● offer a new range of services such as dietary advice and stress counselling
● implement the government's health promotion strategy and its declared intention to shift more hospital services into the community

GP Fundholders were:
● expected to stay within their budgets and avoid unnecessary referrals to hospitals
● able to ensure that their patients benefited from short waiting times by having a wider choice of where to send their patients for treatment than their non-fundholding colleagues

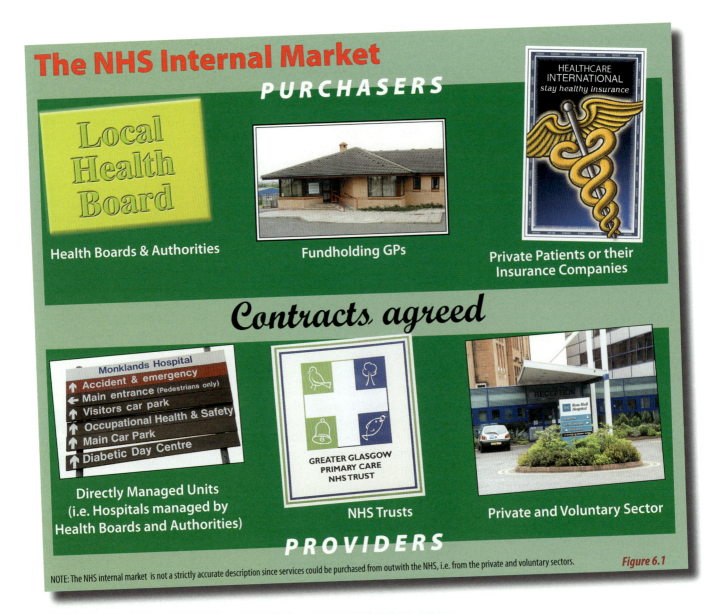

The NHS Internal Market

PURCHASERS

Local Health Board

Health Boards & Authorities

Fundholding GPs

HEALTHCARE INTERNATIONAL *stay healthy insurance*

Private Patients or their Insurance Companies

Contracts agreed

Monklands Hospital
- Accident & emergency
- Main entrance (Pedestrians only)
- Visitors car park
- Occupational Health & Safety
- Main Car Park
- Diabetic Day Centre

Directly Managed Units (i.e. Hospitals managed by Health Boards and Authorities)

GREATER GLASGOW PRIMARY CARE NHS TRUST

NHS Trusts

Private and Voluntary Sector

PROVIDERS

NOTE: The NHS internal market is not a strictly accurate description since services could be purchased from outwith the NHS, i.e. from the private and voluntary sectors.

Figure 6.1

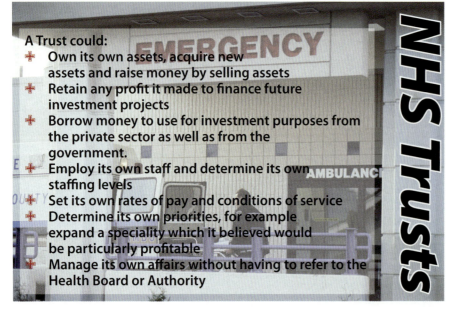

NHS Trusts

A Trust could:
+ Own its own assets, acquire new assets and raise money by selling assets
+ Retain any profit it made to finance future investment projects
+ Borrow money to use for investment purposes from the private sector as well as from the government.
+ Employ its own staff and determine its own staffing levels
+ Set its own rates of pay and conditions of service
+ Determine its own priorities, for example expand a speciality which it believed would be particularly profitable
+ Manage its own affairs without having to refer to the Health Board or Authority

NEW LABOUR AND THE NHS

The election of a Labour government under Tony Blair in 1997 marked the end of eighteen years of Conservative government under Margaret Thatcher and John Major. The Labour government's commitment to modernise the NHS, and to create a Parliament in Scotland and an Assembly in Wales, ensured that further radical reform of the NHS would take place.

The new Labour government abolished the internal market and set up a structure which aimed to build on what had worked previously while discarding what had failed. The goverments's White Paper *The New NHS, Modern and Dependable* put forward a "third way" of running the service based on partnership and driven by performance.

STRUCTURE OF THE NHS (2006)

The creation of a Scottish Parliament in 1999 has enabled the NHS in Scotland to differ in structure from that in England, and also to adopt different strategies for tackling health issues and inequalities. (See opposite.)

Health care in the UK is provided through primary and secondary care. Primary care, as the term suggests, tends to be the first contact the public have with health providers through visits to their doctors, dentists, pharmacists and opticians. This care provides treatment for routine injuries and illnesses and plays an increasing role in preventive care, for example the Paisley health initiative. (See page 90.) Secondary care is associated with visits to hospitals for acute medical care or surgery requirements.

Structure of the NHS in England

Figure 6.3 illustrates the structure of the NHS in England. The Secretary of State for Health decides how the funds allocated by the UK government are to be spent and he or she is responsible to Parliament for the overall performance of the NHS in England. There are three Select Committees in Parliament which can request NHS employees to give evidence to their enquiries.

The Department of Health (DH) is responsible for the running and improvement of the NHS, public

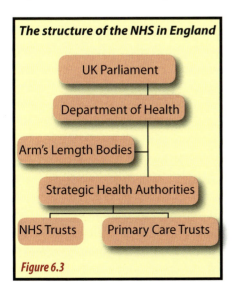

The structure of the NHS in England

- UK Parliament
- Department of Health
- Arm's Lemgth Bodies
- Strategic Health Authorities
- NHS Trusts
- Primary Care Trusts

Figure 6.3

DIFFERENCES BETWEEN SCOTLAND AND ENGLAND

- A single NHS system in Scotland – no NHS Trust Hospitals
- No foundation hospitals – recent health reforms in England have reintroduced the internal market
- Scotland has Community Health Partnerships; England has Primary Care Trusts (PCT's)
- Significantly less involvement of private sector; target in England is to increase private sector delivery of operations from 8% to 15%
- Free Personal Care in Scotland for elderly people who require it
- There is still more per capita health spending in Scotland – England, though, is catching up
- There are still more doctors, nurses and beds in Scotland than in England. Based on population, Scotland has 23% more hospital doctors, 30% more nurses and family doctors

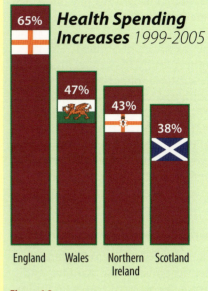

Health Spending Increases 1999-2005

England	Wales	Northern Ireland	Scotland
65%	47%	43%	38%

Figure 6.2 Source: Economic and Social Research Council 2006

NHS CORE PRINCIPLES

In 2000 the Labour government outlined its plans for a patient-centred health service based on the founding principles of the NHS. These can be summed up as follows.

The provision of quality care that:

- meets the needs of every patient
- is free at the point of need
- is based on a patient's clinical need not their ability to pay

The core principles in detail are:

- The NHS will provide a universal service for all based on clinical need, not ability to pay
- The NHS will provide a comprehensive range of services
- The NHS will respond to the different needs of different populations
- The NHS will work together with others to ensure a seamless service for patients
- The NHS will help to keep people healthy and work to reduce health inequalities
- The NHS will provide a universal service for all based on clinical need, not ability to pay

Source: NHS PLAN 2000

health and social care in England. Arm's Length Bodies (ALBs) such as the Modernisation Agency undertake the executive functions of the DH.

The twenty eight Strategic Health Authorities (SHAs) are central to the strategic management of the health service. SHAs monitor the performance of Primary Care Trusts (PCTs) and NHS Trusts, integrate national priorities into local health delivery plans and resolve any conflicts that cannot be resolved between local NHS organisations.

Primary Care Trusts (PCTs)

There are 303 PCTs in England, each responsible for planning and improving primary and community health services in their local areas. The Department of Health has given PCTs the freedom to develop their own targets and frameworks within a set of national standards. PCTs commission secondary care from NHS Trusts, including foundation hospitals, independent (private) hospitals and treatment centres through service level agreements.

NHS Trusts

NHS Trusts employ the majority of the health service's workforce. The creation of foundation hospitals in 2004 has introduced aspects of the internal market created by the Conservatives. (Scotland has not introduced foundation hospitals.) NHS Trusts receive most of their income from service level agreements with their local PCT. Trusts that exceed contractual expectation will receive more funding. However, Trusts that fail to deliver will have their agreements withdrawn and will be regarded as 'failing hospitals'.

The Return of the Internal Market

The creation of foundation hospitals and a new system of 'payment by results' for hospital trusts, which was introduced in 2005, has effectively restored the 'internal market'. The increased role of the private sector (see Chapter 9)

NHS Foundation Trust Hospitals

In April 2004 the first ten foundation hospitals were set up in England and Wales. The Blair government faced strong opposition from its backbench Labour MPs. David Hinchliffe, a Labour MP, stated "that this is a Conservative policy ... and is the internal market all over again. This is the competitive ethos that I thought we had been elected to get rid of." The bill passed the House of Commons in November 2003 by only seventeen votes (Labour's majority in the House of Commons was 160), displaying strong opposition from within Labour.

Delegates to the Labour Party Conference voted against foundation hospitals. It is an issue which divided the party.

Advantages of NHS Foundation Trusts

✔ Hospital managers are not line managed by the Department of Health and have greater control over the running of the hospital. Managers are supported by a board of governors elected from local people, staff and patients; the governors in turn choose the hospital's non-executive directors.

✔ NHS Foundation Trusts are able to borrow money from banks to finance capital programmes and are allowed to retain the proceeds from land sales for reinvestment within the hospital.

✔ NHS Foundation Trusts are able to establish private companies and can pay staff at rates which are over and above nationally agreed terms and conditions

✔ According to the government, foundation hospitals are a halfway house between the public and private sectors—a third way.

✔ They bring efficiency and competition to the NHS and a successful foundation hospital can help to reduce waiting lists.

Disadvantages of NHS Foundation Trusts

✘ They have the potential to create a two-tier NHS and a return to the Conservatives' internal market.

✘ The NHS elite foundation hospitals will get more resources at the expense of failing hospitals, thus widening health inequalities.

✘ They will create staff shortages in non-foundation hospitals as they can 'poach their staff'.

✘ Foundation Hospitals recreate competition between hospitals instead of the cooperation required to ensure that all patients receive the best possible health care.

further confirms a move towards Conservative health policies. Under the new payment system every patient admitted for an elective (non-emergency) operation has a price-tag attached to her/his treatment, so hospitals will be paid according to how busy they are. This will encourage hospitals to cut their costs and become more efficient. The fear is that the ability of Primary Care Trusts to purchase hospital treatment might face a funding crisis if hospitals do more work than they have budgeted for. Hospitals could face bankruptcy if they fail to get enough work or fail to control their costs. The government argues that NHS Foundation Trusts (foundation hospitals) must become more businesslike and is determined in future years to avoid the 2005 – 06 situation whereby the health service ran up a net deficit of £536 million in England and Wales with almost a third of its 600 organisations going into the red. The government is determined to increase the number of NHS hospitals becoming NHS Foundation Trusts which have greater financial autonomy and more incentives to compete.

Structure of the NHS in Scotland (2006)

The Scottish Parliament, through its devolved powers, is responsible for health in Scotland. The Minister of Health and Community Care is accountable to the Scottish Parliament for all health policies and the running of the NHS. The Parliament's Health Committee can call to account the Scottish Executive Health Department's Chief Executive and the chairs of all the NHS Boards. Andy Kerr, the Minister of Health and Community Care in 2006, took drastic action against failing Health Boards. In 2005 the Argyll and Clyde Health Board was dissolved by the Scottish Executive. The Board, which covered an area stretching from Campbeltown to

Renfrew, was £80 million in debt. The solution was for the Scottish Executive to pay off its debts and for the Board's responsibilities to be divided between the new NHS Greater Glasgow and Clyde and NHS Highland.

Figure 6.5 illustrates the structure of the NHS in Scotland. The Scottish Executive Health Department (SEHD) is responsible for delivering health policies and for supervising the work of the Health Boards. The Special Health Boards in Scotland provide services across the country and include NHS 24, NHS Education for Scotland, the Golden Jubilee National hospital, the Scottish Ambulance Service, NHS Health Scotland, NHS Quality Improvement Scotland, and the State hospital Board for Scotland.

The fourteen NHS Health Boards are responsible for allocating funds, developing local health plans—in association with local hospitals and GPs—and taking part in regional and national planning. In 2003 the Scottish White Paper, *Partnership for Care*, was published. This led to the abolition of all Trusts in Scotland, replacing them with operating divisions within the NHS Boards. Each Board has a number of operating divisions which cover primary and secondary care.

Community Health Partnerships (CHPs) are joint organisations made up of local authorities, groups of GPs and other health professionals in a designated geographical area. CHPs integrate health services and are accountable to their NHS Board. Each CHP has a budget to deliver the NHS core principles (see page 69) together with health care in the local community, taking into consideration its own local priorities.

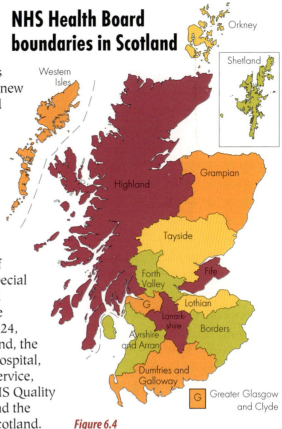

NHS Health Board boundaries in Scotland

Orkney

Shetland

Western Isles

Highland

Grampian

Tayside

Forth Valley

Fife

G

Lothian

Lanarkshire

Borders

Ayrshire and Arran

Dumfries and Galloway

G Greater Glasgow and Clyde

Figure 6.4

The structure of the NHS in Scotland

Scottish Parliament

The Scottish Health Department

Special Health Boards

NHS Health Boards

Operating Divisions

Community Health Partnerships

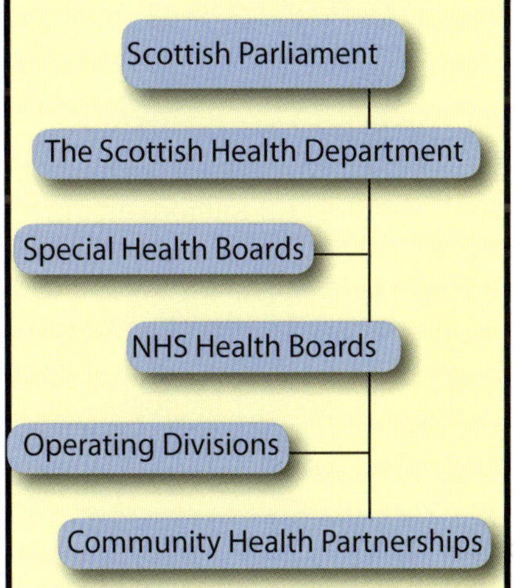

Figure 6.5

Trades & works
1.2%

Technical staff
2.4%

Ancillary
staff
10.6%

Senior
management,
Administration
& Clerical
18.9%

Nursing and
midwifery staff
42.7%

Healthcare science staff
2.5%

Ambulance staff
2.0%

Pharmacy staff
1.3%

Therapeutic staff
7.5%

All
medical
& dental
staff
10.9%

Figure 6.6

The NHS Workforce

Providing a 24-hour service makes the NHS the biggest employer in the UK. Since 1997 the NHS workforce in England has increased from 1 million to to 1.3 million, an increase of 30%. The number of NHS employees in England now stands at a record level with a significant increase in the number of doctors, nurses and managerial posts. The number of managers have almost doubled in the last twelve years and now stands at 40,000.

NHS Scotland Workforce: Selected staff 1995 – 2005		
	1995	2005
Dentists	2,241	2,635
Consultants	2,511	3,480
Nurses	52,416	55,468
Administrative	33,884	37,105

Table 6.1 Source: ISD Scottish National Statistics release 2006

Scotland has also experienced an increase in staff numbers, although not at the same level as England. The NHS Scotland workforce stands at 154,000, a figure which includes part time staff. Table 6.1 highlights the increase in the number of dentists, consultants, nurses and administrative staff in the period 1995 – 2005. Figure 6.6 provides a profile of staffing.This shows that almost half of the staff (42.7%) were in the 'Nursing and midwifery' group.

Chapter 7

Inequalities in health

One of the fundamental principles on which the NHS was based in 1948 was a commitment to remove inequalities in the provision of health care. Yet, despite the achievements of the NHS, there is clear evidence that a person's social position, ethnic origin, sex and the area in which they stay can affect their chances of achieving good health.

There are many influences on an individual's health e.g. biological factors, personal lifestyle, the physical and social environment, and health services. (See Figure 7.1.) For this reason, care must be taken before concluding that geographical, or social class, or other factors are the key to explaining differences in mortality (death) rates or morbidity (illnesses) among individuals or groups.

GEOGRAPHICAL INEQUALITIES

In February 2006 a new Health Inequalities Study by Caci, an information service company, made the headlines in all Scottish newspapers. The system used by Caci measures alcohol consumption, smoking, exercise, weight and long-term illness. It draws on official information, as well as private sector market research, and can identify individual streets with a particularly high concentration of unhealthy residents. The headline in *The Herald* summed up its depressing statistics—"Scotland: sick man of the UK with 22 of the top 25 illness areas". A previous national survey by Bristol University in 1999 (see pages 74–5) had provided similar banner headlines when The *Daily Record* highlighted the North-South

divide—"Shock report reveals the poorest places in Britain are all in Scotland". While both surveys emphasised the geographical divide, the reports clearly identified poverty as being the main culprit. (See page 74.)

There is a clear North-South divide in the health of the British public. According to numerous government statistics, "Death rates are highest in Scotland followed by the north and north-west regions of England, and are lowest in the south-west and eastern regions of England". A 2006 Report by the Commons Public Accounts Committee highlights the wide disparities in cancer care and death rates across the UK. (See Figure 7.2.) Scotland has the highest death rate from lung cancer—98 men and 42 women per 100,000—almost twice the death rate in the South-west. Also life expectancy, for men and women,

Figure 7.1

General socio-economic, cultural and environmental conditions
Living and working conditions
Social and community influences
Individual lifestyle factors
Age, sex & hereditary factors

Factors influencing... health

Health Expenditure by country per head (£) 2003 - 04

England	1085
Scotland	1262
Wales	1186

Table 7.1

Source: Campaign for an English Parliament 2004

Life Expectancy 2004

	Male	Female
Scotland	74	78
United Kingdom	77	81

Table 7.2

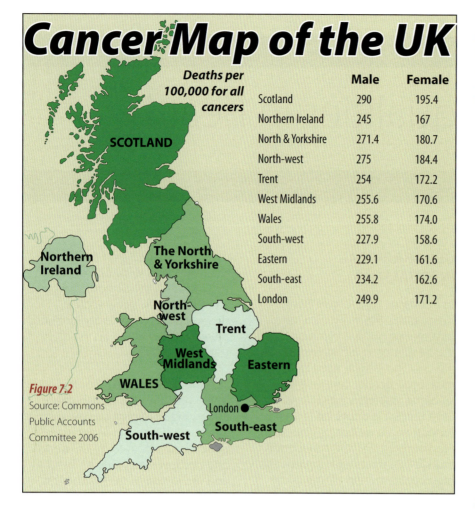

Cancer Map of the UK

Deaths per 100,000 for all cancers	Male	Female
Scotland	290	195.4
Northern Ireland	245	167
North & Yorkshire	271.4	180.7
North-west	275	184.4
Trent	254	172.2
West Midlands	255.6	170.6
Wales	255.8	174.0
South-west	227.9	158.6
Eastern	229.1	161.6
South-east	234.2	162.6
London	249.9	171.2

Figure 7.2
Source: Commons
Public Accounts
Committee 2006

is lower in Scotland compared to the UK average. (See Table 7.2.) This difference cannot be explained through a disparity in health care expenditure and health service employees. In fact, Table 7.1 clearly shows that spending on health in Scotland is significantly higher than in England, yet we experience more ill health. Significantly, spending on the health service in England has increased at a faster rate than in other parts of the UK.

Caci Report 2006

The Caci Report once again confirmed the shockingly unhealthy lifestyles of a significant number of Scots. The Report found that Scots are more likely to suffer long-term illnesses, take less exercise, be more overweight, and spend more on cigarettes and alcohol than other Britons.

By concentrating on precise wards within urban and rural areas, the Report was able to highlight pockets of health deprivation within wealthy areas. Aberdeen, regarded as a prosperous city, had five wards in the UK's top twenty five unhealthy areas. As was expected, Glasgow had six areas in the 'league table' and Dundee three, thus underlining the link between urban deprivation and ill health. Phil Hanlon, Professor of Public Health at Glasgow University, stated:

" This study confirms our efforts are having an effect in some areas, but not in the poorest areas."

The Bowbridge area in Dundee had the dubious honour of being the most unhealthy area in Britain. (See page 75.) All of Britain's twenty five healthiest wards are located in the Home Counties of England with most concentrated in the London commuter belt. Newcastle West (worst area number 13) is England's most unhealthy ward in which spending on tobacco averages £415 a year per person and 47% of residents are overweight.

The Survey once again highlights the north-south health divide. Significantly, all of the worst areas are in run-down housing estates either on the periphery of a city or in an inner city.

Britain's Least Healthy Neighbourhoods

1. Bowbridge, Dundee
2. Greenock Central, Inverclyde
3. Seaton, Aberdeen
4. St James, Renfrewshire
5. Fairmuir, Dundee
6. Sheddocksley, Aberdeen
7. Wyndford, Glasgow
8. Greenock East Central, Inverclyde
9. Garthdee, Aberdeen
10. North Muirton, Perth and Kinross
11. Govan, Glasgow
12. Dennistoun, Glasgow
13. Newcastle West
14. Mastrick, Aberdeen
15. Whitehouse, Newtonabbey
16. Carntyne, Glasgow
17. Seedhill, Renfrewshire
18. Stobswell, Dundee City
19. Hutchesontown, Glasgow
20. South Inch, Perth and Kinross
21. Fraserburgh North, Aberdeenshire
22. Moorside, Newcastle-Upon-Tyne
23. Bridgeton/Dalmarnock, Glasgow
24. Dawson, Falkirk
25. Stockethill, Aberdeen

1999 Bristol University Report

This evidence, produced in December 1999 by researchers from Bristol University, confirmed that the north-south health gap was widening. The researchers compared death and illness rates for infants, children from 1 to 4, and adults under the age of 65 in each of the 641 UK parliamentary constituencies. They also included the following socio-economic statistics: average household income, exam failure rates, unemployment rates and the percentage who were permanently sick. The results made depressing reading for Scotland and especially for Glasgow.

Bowbridge—Dundee

Its lunchtime in the Hawthorn pub in the Bowbridge area of Dundee and the drinks are flowing. Benny is already on his fifth beer and has just made his second visit to the newsagent to buy tobacco. Before the day is out he will have drunk 12 bottles of Newcastle Brown Ale and smoked 60 roll-ups. If he can be bothered eating at all, he may have a roll with crisps—anything more would detract from the serious business of drinking. Benny, in his early forties, is typical of many who live in what has been rewarded the dubious title of Britain's unhealthiest neighbourhood.

Outside, row upon row of bricked-up tenements sit cheek-by-jowl with multi-storey blocks earmarked for demolition. Gangs of hooded youths roam the streets, drinking bottles of fortified wine by the neck and drawing on cigarettes. Every inch of every wall is scrawled with graffiti and desolate stretches of wasteland are strewn with dog mess, rotting mattresses and litter.

"The pub is the real community centre here. There's nothing to do except go the pub. People get bored—they turn to drink, drugs and crime," said Benny.

Bowbridge is one of the 22 areas in Scotland that rank among Britain's unhealthiest, according to one of the most comprehensive studies ever conducted into the nation's well-being. Its residents spend, on average, £486 a year on tobacco, a third have long-term illnesses and only one in four takes part in active sport.

It contrasts starkly with Cheam, in south London, which is the healthiest neighbourhood in Britain. The residents spend on average just £85 per year on tobacco, only 14% suffer from long-term illness and almost 40% participate in sport.

Adapted from *The Sunday Times* 19 February 2006

The six constituencies with the poorest health in Britain were all in Glasgow and the six healthiest constituencies were in the south of England. According to the researchers, the gap between the health of people living in the poorest and those living in the wealthiest areas of Britain was wider than at any time using the death and long-term illness rate. This occured despite the fact that the average health of the population was improving.

People in Shettleston or Springburn were 3.4 times more likely to die before the age of 65 than those in Wokingham or Woodspring, the healthiest areas of south-east England.

The most shocking statistics were the needless deaths of babies. In the Anniesland constituency of Glasgow (which includes Drumchapel) infant mortality rates were 103 deaths per 10,000 births in the first year of life, three times as high as in Woodspring or South Norfolk.

Gerry Spence, a doctor in Shettleston, highlighted unemployment and lifestyle as the culprits. Dr Spence said, "People do not have jobs, they do not have money, and they smoke too much. If people changed their lifestyle, these figures would be dramatically improved. I have seen, very recently, one young woman having a heart attack. As a young woman smoker you are seven times more likely to suffer a heart attack than if you are not a smoker."

LOCAL DIFFERENCES

Recent research in this area, however, has indicated that basing policies on the principle of tackling geographical inequalities is much too simplistic an approach. There are areas in Scotland and Northern Ireland, for instance, which compare favourably with the healthiest areas in the south-east of England, while there are parts of London which have records of poor health comparable to the most deprived areas in the country.

It is clear that social class and lifestyle play a crucial role. This is clearly highlighted in Table 7.3.

The social class divide is clear in terms of homeowners (double in Strathkelvin and Bearsden compared to Shettleston) and in academic qualifications. There is also a clear link between unhealthy lifestyles—smoking, alcohol and drugs—and health in terms of heart and cancer deaths and long-term illnesses. The contrast between Strathkelvin and Bearsden and Shettleston is stark.

SOCIAL CLASS INEQUALITIES

The Black Report

Numerous reports have highlighted the link between poverty and poor health. The most famous was the Black Report in 1980 and unfortunately most recent reports confirm that its findings are still relevant today.

This enquiry into *Inequalities in Health* established for the first time a clear link between different socio economic groups and health. Sir Douglas Black, President of the Royal College of Physicians, used the classifications defined by the Registrar General. The Black Report concluded that while the health of the nation had improved, inequalities in health between the higher and lower social classes was widening. Class inequalities in health could be traced from childhood and continued throughout life.

The Report concluded that the government should take a more active role in encouraging changes "in people's diet, exercise and smoking and drinking behaviour. Greater emphasis should be given to preventing ill health rather than curing it and a first step should be a ban on smoking in public places." (See page 89.)

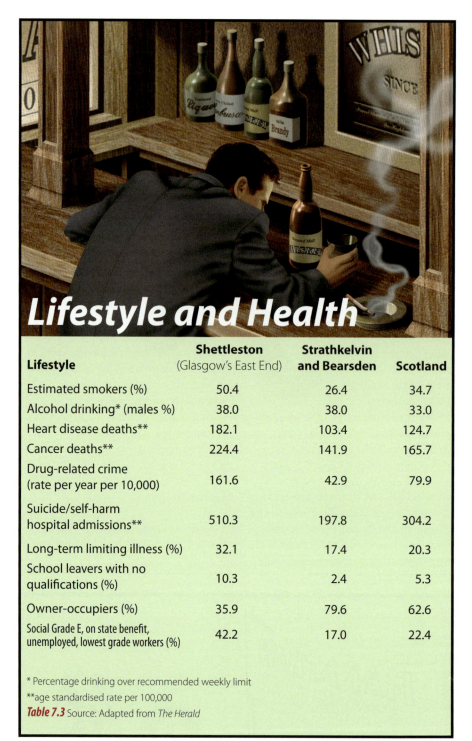

Lifestyle and Health

Lifestyle	Shettleston (Glasgow's East End)	Strathkelvin and Bearsden	Scotland
Estimated smokers (%)	50.4	26.4	34.7
Alcohol drinking* (males %)	38.0	38.0	33.0
Heart disease deaths**	182.1	103.4	124.7
Cancer deaths**	224.4	141.9	165.7
Drug-related crime (rate per year per 10,000)	161.6	42.9	79.9
Suicide/self-harm hospital admissions**	510.3	197.8	304.2
Long-term limiting illness (%)	32.1	17.4	20.3
School leavers with no qualifications (%)	10.3	2.4	5.3
Owner-occupiers (%)	35.9	79.6	62.6
Social Grade E, on state benefit, unemployed, lowest grade workers (%)	42.2	17.0	22.4

* Percentage drinking over recommended weekly limit

**age standardised rate per 100,000

Table 7.3 Source: Adapted from *The Herald*

Health Survey for England 1998

This was published in January 1998 and was the first official government acknowledgement since the Black Report that geography, wealth and class make a difference to health. The Report highlighted that people from deprived urban areas are far more likely to smoke and to suffer generally poor health, asthma, obesity and high blood pressure than those in better off areas.

Based on interviews and medicals involving more than 17,000 adults and 3,000 children, the survey showed that:

- more women are drinking beyond safe limits

- more young men in the 16–34 age group are smoking than in other age groups

- the number of obese people is increasing, especially among women

The 1998 Acheson Report

In 1997 the new Labour government set up a Commission under the chairmanship of Sir Donald Acheson, the former Chief Medical Officer for England and Wales, to investigate health inequalities in the United Kingdom.

The Report provided a comprehensive survey of the condition of the disadvantaged and its conclusion echoed the Black Report—poverty had to be tackled through concerted government action and a policy of social inclusion in education, housing, employment, social services and health provision.

The Report summarised the lives of nine million adults and two million children in the following way.

> "The poor were unhealthy. They did not live as long and they suffered more from lung cancer, coronary heart disease, strokes, suicide and violent accidents than their richer peers. These inequalities had steadily worsened over the preceding twenty years. They were more likely to have their cars stolen and their homes vandalised. They ate less iron, calcium, dietary fibre and vitamin C. They were fatter."

Their homes were colder. There has been little significant improvement since the Acheson Report was published.

Centre for Population Studies

Recent research indicates that the cycle and extent of poverty has a biological effect which means that generations of families who live in areas of deprivation are more likely to succumb to illness. This is one hypothesis that Glasgow Centre for Population, which is running the study, is trying to test. Scientific links between physiological changes, such as tissue inflammation, and mental tension are being investigated. A separate report by a group of researchers on *Geographical Variation in Mortality by Social Class* provides some evidence to support the above hypothesis. (See Figure 7.3.) What is interesting

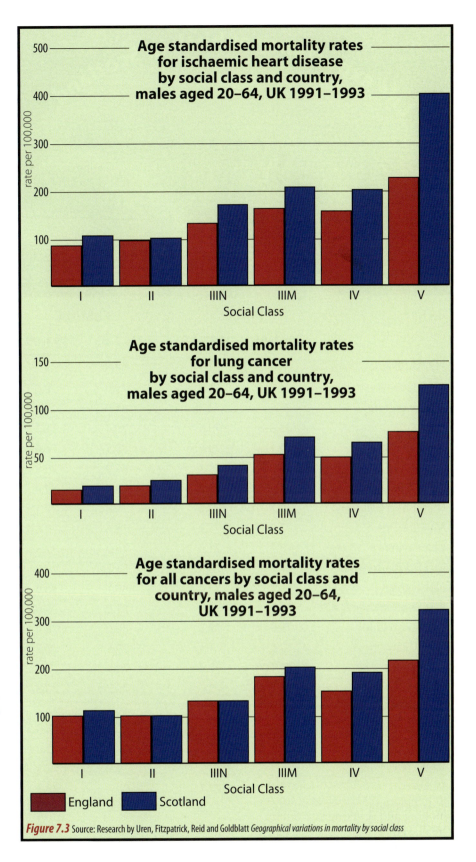

Figure 7.3 Source: Research by Uren, Fitzpatrick, Reid and Goldblatt *Geographical variations in mortality by social class*

about this report is that it uses socio-economic status to compare mortality rates across the United Kingdom.

The most significant finding is the variation across the UK in health for social class V (the group most likely to suffer from poverty). The social class V figure for heart disease is almost double in Scotland compared to that of England, while the Scottish figure is significantly greater for all cancers. A key question is why, coming from a similar poor socio-economic background, is the health of the Scots so much worse?

77

Life expectancy at birth in Scotland

Table 7.4 Source: Registrar General for Scotland

	MALE		FEMALE	
	2003–05	**1993–95**	**2003–05**	**1993–95**
SCOTLAND	**74.2**	**71.9**	**79.2**	**77.5**
Aberdeen City	74.9	73.2	79.9	78.0
Aberdeenshire	76.7	74.3	81.0	79.0
Angus	75.8	73.5	79.4	78.1
Argyll & Bute	75.1	71.6	80.7	78.0
Borders	75.8	71.1	80.0	78.9
Clackmannanshire	73.2	73.0	78.7	77.4
Dumfries & Galloway	75.7	73.3	79.8	78.1
Dundee City	73.0	71.1	78.4	77.6
East Ayrshire	73.7	71.4	78.0	77.3
East Dunbartonshire	77.7	74.9	81.2	78.8
East Lothian	76.1	73.4	80.1	78.6
East Renfrewshire	76.8	74.9	81.0	79.5
Edinburgh City	75.5	72.5	80.6	78.4
Eilean Siar	72.1	71.3	79.5	78.2
Falkirk	74.4	72.4	79.1	77.1
Fife	75.4	73.0	79.7	78.3
Glasgow City	69.9	67.9	76.7	75.2
Highland	75.0	72.3	80.3	78.4
Inverclyde	71.1	69.0	77.9	75.8
Midlothian	75.2	73.2	79.5	77.3
Moray	75.6	72.7	80.1	78.3
North Ayrshire	73.8	71.6	78.9	76.9
North Lanarkshire	72.7	70.8	77.6	76.1
Orkney Islands	76.3	73.3	81.4	79.2
Perth & Kinross	76.4	73.2	80.6	78.0
Renfrewshire	72.6	71.4	78.2	77.1
Shetland Islands	75.3	71.1	81.0	78.5
South Ayrshire	75.0	73.1	80.1	77.9
South Lanarkshire	74.3	71.7	79.1	77.0
Stirling	76.3	72.9	80.1	78.6
West Dunbartonshire	71.0	70.9	77.5	76.5
West Lothian	74.3	72.0	78.4	77.5

LIFE EXPECTANCY GAP IS WIDENING

Figures released by the Registrar General for Scotland in September 2006 further confirmed that the disparity in health between people in the richest and poorest areas had widened over the preceding decade.

The people who live longest in Scotland live in East Dunbartonshire, just a few miles from the boundaries of Glasgow which has the lowest life expectancy and is the only authority where the figure for men is under 70. In contrast the male figure for East Dunbartonshire is 77.7. A woman in East Dunbartonshire has a life expectancy of 81.2, while the figure for a woman in Glasgow is 76.7.

On the positive side the statistics conclude that the people of Scotland, including those in Glasgow, are living longer and that the gap between the sexes has narrowed to just five years. Overall life expectancy for the sexes has increased to 74.2 and 79.2 for men and women respectively.

A spokesperson for the Scottish Executive welcomed the overall improvement in health while stating that "the main problem is persistent health inequalities across Scotland, and improving everyone's health while tackling these inequalities is the main aim of our health improvement policies". (See Chapter 8.)

LIFESTYLE ISSUES

OBESITY AND BAD DIET

A recent international report on obesity in young people paints a depressing picture of youth in Scotland. The rise in the number of overweight children is a phenomenon common to the Western world, and is based on a diet of high fat junk food and a dramatic reduction in physical activity. Furthermore, the international report reveals that Scottish boys are growing fatter than their counterparts in England and are heading towards becoming the fattest in Europe. One in eight Scots children is classified as officially overweight.

The energy imbalance is widened by the reduction in exercise. Average energy expenditure among children is estimated to have fallen by 800 calories a day since the 1950s, but the proportion of fat in the diet has soared by 50%. These findings reflect the scientific view that not only is the population at large getting fatter, it is getting fatter younger. Dr Andrew Prentice of the Dunn Clinical Nutrition Centre in Cambridge states that the rising levels of obesity are a reflection of general changes in society. With children it is now a matter of "stopping them going down the same road as their mums and dads have already gone." Children with two obese parents run a 70% risk of becoming obese, compared with a risk of less than 20% among children with two lean parents.

In 1996 10% of children in the UK were obese with the figure increasing to 16% by 2004.

Social Class and Obesity

A careful examination of the socio-economic distribution of those in Britain who are overweight confirms that fat is also a class issue. The lowest social class has levels of obesity which match American levels, while the highest social class has the lowest obesity levels. This contrasts with the traditional concept of deprivation which sees the poor as being very pale and thin and the wealthy as 'fat cats'.

Obesity is referred to as a disease of prosperity and over the last twenty years more and more Britons have become dangerously overweight. Obesity is linked to heart disease, diabetes and premature death.

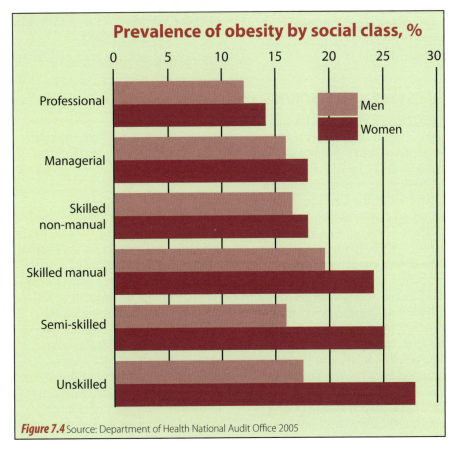

Figure 7.4 Source: Department of Health National Audit Office 2005

This image stems from pictures in the media of deprivation in the developing world.

Figure 7.4 illustrates the link between social class and obesity, especially among women. The number of unskilled women who are obsese is a staggering 28%, double the figure for professional women. It is also significant that in every social class more women are obese than men.

Lifestyle plays a crucial part in explaining these differences. Nutritionists agree that inactivity rather than diet is the key element in obesity. According to Mike Lean, Professor of Human Nutrition at Glasgow University, "People in what used to be called the manual working classes view physical activity as something they have to do and they hate it. The minute they stop work they put their feet up ... whereas people in social classes I and II take great pride in demonstrating their physique by jogging and weekend activites."

Our changing diet is also a contributory factor. High fat food, of which we are consuming 50% more than in the 1960s, has replaced sugar as the main cause of people being overweight. Fat contains twice the calories of protein and carbohydrate.

LIFESTYLE AND SMOKING

Smoking is a crucial factor in the ill health of people who live in deprived areas. Smoking is a class issue as Table 7.6 illustrates. In 1958 there was no significant difference in the smoking habits of all social classes for both men and women. Smoking was regarded as an acceptable habit and was not linked with cancer and other health problems. By the 1990s the professional classes has listened to health advice and the number of male smokers in social class I had fallen by 75%. In contrast, the number of smokers in social class V had only dropped by 30%. The figures for women in the lower socio-economic groups displayed a drop of only about 10%, despite all the health

While the health of both males and females is improving, the rate of improvement is greater for men. Smoking, alcohol consumption and obesity are key factors, as outlined in the official statistics below.

The convergence of male and female life expectancy appears to be linked to converging lifestyles.

Smoking: From 1974 to 2002 (latest data) the decline in the number of men smoking (from 51% to 28%) has been greater than that of women (41% to 26%).

Drinking: Alcohol consumption in excess of the number of recommended weekly units is commoner among men than women (7% of adult males and 3% of females in 2002) and is highest in the 16–24 age category (12% of males and 10% of females in 2002) . However, drinking to excess has risen much more quickly among women than men in recent years, particularly among 16 to 24-year-olds where between 1988 and 2002 levels of excess drinking rose from 3% to 10% of women versus a rise from 10% to 12% among men.

Obesity: The proportion of the population with a body mass index (BMI) of over 30* continues to rise and women are more likely to be obese than men. In 1994, 15% of adult males and 18% of adult females were officially obese. By 2002, 21% of males and 22% of females were obese. For the first time levels of male obesity are starting to catch up with levels of female obesity.

(According to the Department of Health guidelines a BMI index over 30 is obese.)

Source: Office of Health Economics 2006

GENDER LIFESTYLE ISSUES

campaigns. It is women, especially young women, who are the most vulnerable.

A smoking time bomb

A time bomb is ticking which, in the long run, will impact on the lifespan of females. The number of 15-year-old girls who say they smoke every day has doubled in recent years. Professor Stephen Spiro stated that Glasgow had one of the worst records for lung cancer among women. He said, "More women die from lung cancer in Glasgow and Liverpool than anywhere else in the UK. Women are twenty years behind men in their smoking

habits. Men were struck down with vicious (lung) cancer years ago and now the pattern is moving on. It is women who will now be experiencing this vicious type of lung cancer." (See page 81.)

It is clear that smoking is one factor which explains the different mortality rates between the social classes. When one examines Table 7.5 which identifies areas with the highest and lowest proportions of people smoking, the social class differences are stark. All of the highest areas are in areas of poor health and poverty and all of the lowest areas are in areas of excellent health and prosperity.

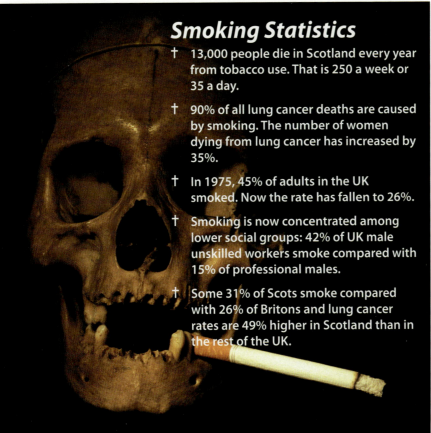

Smoking Statistics

† 13,000 people die in Scotland every year from tobacco use. That is 250 a week or 35 a day.

† 90% of all lung cancer deaths are caused by smoking. The number of women dying from lung cancer has increased by 35%.

† In 1975, 45% of adults in the UK smoked. Now the rate has fallen to 26%.

† Smoking is now concentrated among lower social groups: 42% of UK male unskilled workers smoke compared with 15% of professional males.

† Some 31% of Scots smoke compared with 26% of Britons and lung cancer rates are 49% higher in Scotland than in the rest of the UK.

Areas with the Highest Proportion of Smoking (Scotland) (%)

1	G52	Hillington, Glasgow	45.1
2	G22	Milton, Glasgow	44.4
3	G53	Nitshill, Glasgow	44.0
4	G53	Pollok, Glasgow	43.5
5	EH11	East Hermiston, Edinburgh	43.2

Areas with lowest proportion of smoking (%)

1	EH54	Murieston, Edinburgh	19.1
2	G74	Thorntonhall, Glasgow	19.7
3	G76	Clarkston, Glasgow	20.1
4	TD12	Coldstream, Galashiels	20.1
5	AB13	Milltimber, Aberdeen	20.6

Table 7.5

Prevalence of cigarette smoking:
by sex and selected socio-economic classification (2004–2005)

	Men	Women
Managerial and Professional		
Higher professional occupations	16	11
Lower professional and managerial occupations	22	20
Intermediate		
Intermediate occupations	26	22
Small employers/ own account workers	25	20
Routine and Manual semi-routine occupations	34	30
Routine Occupations	33	33

Table 7.6 Source: General Household Survey Office for National Statistics (2006)

ALCOHOL ABUSE

Excessive consumption of alcohol leads to ill health with an increased likelihood of illnesses such as cirrhosis of the liver and high blood pressure. Parts of Scotland are blighted by a booze culture which, according to the NHS, kills forty Scots a week.

Total recorded alcohol consumption doubled in the UK between 1962 and 2002. A 2006 *Report of Alcohol Trends in Scotland* painted a depressing picture. It estimated that deaths linked to drinking alcohol would subsequently double over twenty years. In the 1980s there were around 200 deaths related to alcohol in Greater Glasgow every year. The 2005 figure had risen to about 500 and the report warned that unless trends change there will be almost 1,000 by 2026. (See Figure 7.5.) Table 7.8 illustrates that more males than females suffer from alcohol problems. There are also significant regional differences. The Western Isles, followed by Glasgow and Inverclyde have the highest figures, with East Dunbartonshire and Abberdeenshire the lowest.

A further major concern is the increase in young people, especially teenagers, who drink to excess. (See page 82.) Ian Gilmore, of the Royal College of Physicians, stated that it had once been unusual to see serious alcohol-related liver damage before the age of 40. Now people in their 30s or even in their 20s are showing signs of such damage. The youngest person found to have alcohol-related liver damage was a 17-year-old who started drinking at the age of 12.

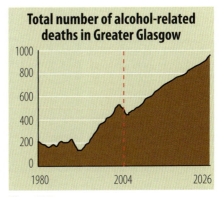

Total number of alcohol-related deaths in Greater Glasgow

Figure 7.5

81

Teenage Binge Drinking

There are grave health concerns over the rise of binge drinking by teenagers, especially girls. A European Schools Survey Project on Alcohol and Drugs (ESPAD), which included more than 100,000 European students, found that teenage girls in the UK are now bigger binge drinkers than boys. (See Table 7.7.) The headline in *The Herald* newspaper reporting on the above survey was "Ladette drinkers outstrip the boys." The only other country where more girls admitted binge drinking was Ireland (33% to the UK's 29%). When the last ESPAD survey was carried out in 1999, 33% of 15 and 16-year-old boys and 27% of girls were binge drinkers.

Teenage Binge* Drinking 2003,% (selected countries)

	All Teenagers	Boys	Girls
Italy	13	19	8
Greece	11	14	8
Norway	24	31	18
UK	27	26	29
Ireland	32	31	33
France	9	13	7

*Binge drinking was classified as having more than five alcoholic drinks in a row at least three times in the preceding thirty days.

Table 7.7 Source: European School Survey Project on Alcohol and Drugs 2004

Hospital discharge rate per 100,000 population with alcohol-related problems
(Scotland and selected authorities)

Authority	Male	Female
Aberdeen City	1278	475
Aberdeenshire	564	274
West Dunbartonshire	1456	416
Dundee City	997	371
East Dunbartonshire	515	150
East Lothian	721	393
City of Edinburgh	904	390
City of Glasgow	2316	646
Highland	1376	522
Inverclyde	2127	477
North Ayrshire	1441	610
North Lanarkshire	1170	356
Perth and Kinross	651	244
Renfrewshire	1383	405
Western Isles	2332	780
Scotland	748	407

Table 7.8 Source: NHS Statistics Division Scotland 2006

GENDER INEQUALITIES

The gender gap in health was summarised by Miles in 1991:

> "Women live longer but suffer from more health problems in their lifetime."

Mortality rates

As you can see from Figure 7.6, life expectancy has significantly increased over the last seventy five years. The data also shows that in 2004 life expectancy for a woman at birth was four years longer than for a man.

More males than females are born each year; nearly 368,000 boys were born in the UK in 2004 compared with 348,000 girls. However, overall there were more females than males in the UK—30.6 million and 29.3 million respectively.

Figure 7.7 is explained by the higher level of male deaths in every age group from birth through to adulthood.

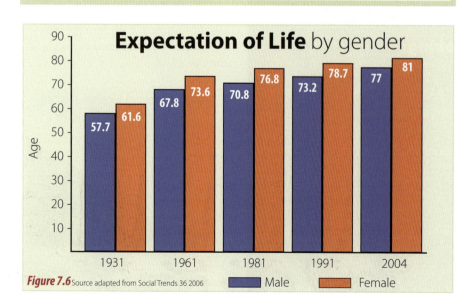

Expectation of Life by gender

Year	Male	Female
1931	57.7	61.6
1961	67.8	73.6
1981	70.8	76.8
1991	73.2	78.7
2004	77	81

Figure 7.6 Source adapted from Social Trends 36 2006

■ Male   ■ Female

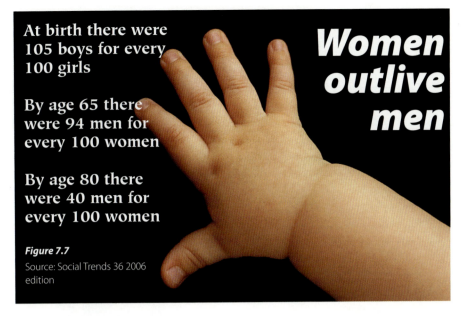

At birth there were 105 boys for every 100 girls

By age 65 there were 94 men for every 100 women

By age 80 there were 40 men for every 100 women

Women outlive men

Figure 7.7

Source: Social Trends 36 2006 edition

The causes of death, moreover, vary between men and women for different age groups. In the 1–14 age group, for instance, nearly twice as many boys as girls die from accidents and violence, while in middle age, deaths from lung cancer, heart disease, accidents and suicide are the major reasons for males' higher mortality rates.

In Scotland, the major cause of death in women is lung cancer rather than breast cancer. While breast cancer is still more common, the recovery rate is far higher than for lung cancer. The smoking habits of young girls are causing concern and there is a fear that the number of females who die from lung cancer will increase.

Research has found that although life expectancy is increasing, healthy life expectancy remained virtually constant between 1980 and 2000 at around 59 years for men and 62 years for women. Thus, the extra years of life create their own problems.

Morbidity rate

Whilst women live longer, they also suffer from more ill health than men. As is the case with men, however, certain groups of women suffer more illness than others. Figures in the General Household Survey suggest that women in the lowest social class group report more than twice the rate of illness as women in the highest group.

Employment status seems to be another factor affecting women's health. With regard to women with children, middle-class women who have paid employment suffer less illness than women from the same class who stay at home, while working-class women with a paid job have worse health than those who do not. Finally, women appear to suffer disproportionately from mental illness, although fewer single women have psychiatric problems than married women. For males the reverse is true—mental health tends to be best among married men.

Towards an Explanation?

Why do women suffer from more health problems than men? Although surveys have suggested that women are more likely to admit to and report illness, three other factors have been highlighted as being more significant explanations.

Biological: Women's role in human reproduction can cause ill health. Pregnancy, childbirth, menstruation, contraception, abortion and the menopause all play a part in the greater morbidity rate experienced by women. This is perhaps borne out by the fact that in the younger age groups more males than females report long-standing illness and this trend is only reversed in the fifteen plus age groups. The increase in the rates of lung cancer among women, at a time when they are beginning to show a decline among men, suggests that sex differences in morbidity may widen while differences in mortality may narrow.

Material: The link between poverty and ill health is well documented, and there is evidence to suggest that women are more likely to suffer from the effects of poverty than men. The reasons for this can be found in women's position in our society. For example, women may have to accept low paid jobs, head one parent families, and may be expected to take on the caring role for elderly and disabled relatives.

Ageing: 70% of those aged over 75 in the UK are women. Since the elderly experience more ill health than those in younger age groups, it is hardly surprising that proportionately women should have higher rates of morbidity than men.

Gender gap closing

The change in lifestyle (see page 80) among females explains why the gap between female and male life expectancy is closing. This convergence is highlighted in Table 7.9.

The death rates from all cancers together has fallen twice as fast for men as for women. While the male lung cancer death rate halved between 1973 and 2003 (-51%), female lung cancer deaths increased by 45%.

Percentage change in age standardised mortality rate, England and Wales, Percentage change 1973–2003		
	Males	**Females**
All causes	-42	-34
All cancers	-21	-10
Lung cancer	-51	45
Coronary heart disease	-57	-54

Table 7.9

ETHNIC INEQUALITIES

In general ethnic minorities, who in 2001 made up 8% of the population, have a younger age structure than the white groups. The mixed groups have the youngest age profile, half being under 16, followed by the Bangladeshis (38%).

In general terms, ethnic minorities suffer the same threats to their health as the rest of the population—circulatory diseases and cancer are the same killers regardless of their ethnic background. However, there is significant variation within the different ethnic communities. The Asian community is more likely to suffer from coronary heart disease, the rate being about 60% higher than for men in the general population. Those of Caribbean extraction, along with the Asian and African communities, are more at risk from strokes compared with the national average.

Asians also have a much higher than average rate of tuberculosis infection. There is a high incidence of diabetes in West Indian and Asian communities. Furthermore, there are higher reported rates of mental illness in the Caribbean community, the incidence of schizophrenia, for example, being higher than among the general population. In addition, there are a number of diseases which are rarely found in Britain outside certain ethnic groups, such as sickle-cell anaemia (Afro-Caribbeans) and rickets (in Asian people). Table 7.11 indicates that infant mortality rates are particularly high for babies born to mothers of Pakistani and Caribbean origin.

Given that excessive alcohol consumption is detrimental to health (see page 81), the ethnic minority groups have an excellent record of non-drinking. (See Table 7.10.) All ethnic minority groups are less likely to drink alcohol than the general population.

Obviously factors such as social class, diet, living standards and levels of poverty impact on the health of all individuals and it is

difficult therefore to explain the above variations in the health of ethnic minorities. One school of thought is that racism has a direct impact upon the health of ethnic minority groups.

If certain groups of people are denied equality of opportunity in areas such as jobs and housing, it is to be expected that this will result in a higher incidence of poverty and that they will experience more ill health than the rest of the population.

The Health of Ethnic Minority Groups

good news

✔ Cancer mortality is lower among all the ethnic minority groups compared with the general population.

✔ Most ethnic minority groups experience lower mortality rates from chronic bronchitis than the general UK population.

✔ People from the Caribbean have much lower rates of heart disease than the general population.

✔ Ethnic Minorities have a lower alcohol consumption rate than the general UK population and have a higher proportion of non-drinkers.

bad news

✘ Infant mortality is higher in the Asian, African and Caribbean communities.

✘ There is a 36% extra risk of heart disease for men born on the Indian sub-continent, and a 46% extra risk for women, compared with rates for England and Wales as a whole.

✘ Caribbean men face a 76% greater risk of suffering a stroke than the general population, and the women's risk is more than double at 110%.

✘ Asians have five times the rates of diabetes as the general population and people from the Caribbean twice that level.

✘ Rates of tuberculosis in Indian, Pakistani and Bangladeshi people in the UK are twenty five times the rate of infection in the general population.

✘ The genetic disorder sickle-cell anaemia particularly affects people from the Caribbean.

Non-Drinkers (%)

	Men	Women
General Population	7	12
Caribbean	7	12
Indian	13	18
Bangladeshi	96	99
Pakistani	91	97
Chinese	30	41

Table 7.10 Source: Social Trends 36 2006

Infant mortality
Infant deaths per 1000 births

UK average	7.8
India	10.6
Pakistan	14.5
Bangladesh	10.5
Caribbean	15.4

Table 7.11 Source: Health survey for England 2003

AGE

By definition, age is a factor in health inequalities. As people age they are more likely to experience a long-standing illness or disability. Chronic health problems include arthritis, rheumatism, heart conditions and dementia. The Alzheimer's society estimates that 98% of the 750,000 people in the UK with dementia are over 65. Dementia affects about one in five of the over-80s and one in twenty of those aged between 65 and 79.

Like the population as a whole the elderly are a varied collection of people. There are also considerable variations between men and women, between different areas of the country and between different ethnic groups.

Furthermore, the Black Report suggested that inequalities in health among the elderly are also the result of differences in social class. Table 7.12 illustrates this association between occupational class and the health of the elderly.

The elderly are key players in the debate over the provision and delivery of health policies. (See pages 104 – 105.)

Customer service assistant at Tesco, Dick Stanners, 82, helps June Sullivan with her shopping. He demonstrates that the elderly are not a homogeneous group as many are capable of and wish to work beyond the recognised retirement age.

Chronic Sickness

Reported long-standing illness by sex, age and socio-economic group (UK 2002)

Socio-economic group of head of household	Male 65+	Female 65+
Professional	48	59
Employers and Managers	55	59
Intermediate Non-manual	62	62
Skilled manual	64	64
Unskilled manual	66	65

Table 7.12

Chapter 8

Policies and strategies to deal with inequalities in health

INDIVIDUAL AND COLLECTIVIST APPROACHES

The Thatcher and Major Conservative governments (1979–1997) denied that material inequalities caused ill health. While accepting the existence of health differences, they concluded that the variations between the health of different social classes could be explained in other ways. They argued that the behaviour of individuals within the social class shaped their health. Poor diet, lack of exercise, heavy smoking and heavy drinking by individuals were to blame, not social class.

Numerous reports, such as the Black Report, which clearly linked social class and health were ignored. The Conservatives regarded the role of the government as being to inform people of the consequences of an inappropriate lifestyle and to offer advice on health improvement. Individualists believe that the post-war 'nanny state' has created a climate where individuals fail to take responsibility for their actions. They also favour greater private provision and greater dependency on individuals to provide for their own health care.

The Labour government elected in 1997 favoured a more collectivist approach and recognised the link between poverty and ill health. This was reinforced by the findings of the Acheson Report commissioned by the new government. (See page 77.)

This chapter will consider the measures taken by the government

to tackle some of the key problems identified in Chapter 7, namely social class and gender health inequalities and the problems associated with smoking, drinking and obesity. There have been some differences in approach between Scotland and England and these will also be considered.

TACKLING SCOTLAND'S HEALTH PROBLEMS

In 1999 Scotland's restored parliament placed the issue of health inequalities high on its political agenda. It was guided by the 1998 Green Paper on Public Health, *Working Together for a Healthier Scotland*, and the 1999 National Review of Resource Allocation for the NHS in Scotland.

Working Together For a Healthier Scotland

In the foreword to the Green Paper Donald Dewar, the Secretary of State for Scotland at the time declared, "Our attack on ill health is a central part of our battle against social exclusion. Ill health and social exclusion are bound up together—ill health can stop you getting a job, for example, and being excluded can damage your health further. That's why the Scottish Office team and I will do all we can to beat ill health—and to beat social exclusion."

The Green Paper set out an action plan of cooperation between health authorities and local government which would tackle health, housing, education and environmental problems. The lottery would

provide £300 million to set up Healthy Living Centres in deprived areas in an attempt to reduce heart disease, cancer and smoking among the disadvantaged. Sam Galbraith, Scottish Health Minister in 1999, highlighted the contrasting health records of Bearsden and Drumchapel. He stated, "Early deaths in Bearsden were 40% below the national average, while in neighbouring Drumchapel they were 60% above. These figures are compelling proof that deprivation is linked to ill health."

Sam Galbraith also placed the Green Paper in the wider context of Labour's New Deal and Social Inclusion policy. Extra funding had been provided for the unemployed, housing, education and health. (See Chapter 5.)

The Conservative Party in Scotland continued to deny the link between poverty and sickness. Mary Scanlan, health spokesperson for the Scottish Conservatives, said, "I think it is wrong to say that poor health is directly linked to poverty and low incomes. It is linked with poor eating and lifestyle habits which can be changed with greater public awareness."

FAIR SHARES FOR ALL

The Arbuthnott formula, based on the 1999 National Review of Resource Allocation for the NHS in Scotland, plays a key role in tackling health inequalities. In 1999 the independent group reviewing Scottish health services, headed by Professor Arbuthnott, introduced a new funding allocation

(Continued on page 88)

WORKING TOGETHER FOR A HEALTHIER SCOTLAND

This Green Paper was a consultation document which set out a wide range of suggestions on how we might all work together towards better health and well-being in Scotland.

The Way Forward

"Improvement in the health of Scots is unlikely to happen by only changing our lifestyles such as, for example, stopping smoking, eating more healthily, drinking less alcohol, taking more exercise. Action is needed as well to tackle those 'life circumstances' which can cause ill health. These are things such as poverty, poor housing, unemployment, poor environment and poor education—things which the previous government chose to ignore as having an effect on our health."

This will be achieved at three levels.

"First, dealing with those 'life circumstances' which give rise to bad health, and encouraging those which lead to good health including a job, decent housing, a good education and a safe and attractive environment in which to live and work. Involving and supporting communities will be a crucial step in the government's efforts to promote health.

Second, to help people change those lifestyles which result in bad health. This will be done by increasing health education on topics such as smoking, diet, physical exercise and alcohol and drug abuse. But the government does not propose to do it in a nagging or nannying way but by encouraging people to make healthy choices that really do improve their quality of life.

Third, to tackle a number of priority health topics, in particular cancer, coronary heart disease, stroke, dental and oral health … The government thinks the best way of doing this is by bringing home to everybody the extent to which illness and early death are preventable."

The following strategies/support will be put in place:

1. Health impact assessment will be used by the government and local authorities on all major policies such as housing.

2. Creation of a public health post in the Convention of Scottish Local Authorities (COSLA) to help develop and coordinate 'healthy' local authorities policies.

3. Creation of a special unit to help develop health education and promotion in schools.

4. Creation of a network of Healthy Living Centres around Scotland, funded from the lottery, to promote good health, in particular within disadvantaged communities. The Centres will help improve people's diet, encourage them to exercise regularly and raise awareness of the country's biggest killers—heart disease, cancer and strokes.

Setting HEALTH targets

The following health targets were set:
Top priority is to reduce premature mortality from coronary heart disease by half and from cancer by 20% in the next ten years, saving the equivalent of more than 2,500 lives in Scotland each year.

SMOKING

Plans to cut smoking among 12- to 15-year-olds, now at its highest level since 1984, from 14% to 11% by 2010. Attempts to reduce the proportion of women smoking during pregnancy from 29% to 20% will also be made. Nicotine substitutes to be provided as free prescriptions and a new law to be considered on banning tobacco advertising.

DRINKING

This is on the increase but there will be a renewed effort to reduce the incidence of men and women exceeding weekly alcohol limits from 33% to 29%, and 13% to 11%, respectively. Reducing the percentage of young people drinking, from 20% to 16%, will form part of a more general drive to improve children's health.

TEENAGE PREGNANCY

It is hoped to cut these rates, which are the highest in Europe, by 20%.

DENTAL DISEASE

By 2010 it is also hoped that 60% of 5-year-old children will have no experience of dental disease. (Fluoridation of the water supply should be considered.)

EXERCISE

It is proposed that half of children aged 12 to 15 should be taking vigorous exercise four times a week, while 60% of men and 50% of women should be taking 30 minutes of exercise five times a week.

which benefits Scotland's poorest areas and rural communities. (See extract from the report.) The Health Minister at the time, Ms Susan Deacon, insisted there would be "no losers" as every Health Board would witness a "real-term increase in growth".

However, not all Health Boards are happy with the formula. In July 2006 NHS Grampian declared that the present funding formula was "morally and ethically unacceptable because Boards such as Glasgow and Clyde are being financially rewarded for unhealthy lifestyles". NHS Grampian receives the lowest per capita allocation of all the health authorities. Grampian has 10.3% of the Scottish population, but receives only 9.0% of NHS funding. While Grampian is regarded as an area of prosperity, Aberdeen suffers from inner city deprivation which impacts on health. (See page 74.)

A Scottish Executive spokesperson stated, "No Board has lost out in recent years and every one has had above inflation funding increases. NHS Grampian's funding is 35% higher at £177 million than five years ago. It is entirely right that health resources go where they are needed most—where people are sicker or older."

WHAT HAS BEEN ACHIEVED?

This section will examine the impact of the above policies and strategies in tackling health inequalities. Vigorous and controversial measures have been taken against smoking and tackling obesity, especially in the young, and binge drinking is a high priority. The decision to restrict smoking has led some health specialists to advocate greater government intervention in controlling the drinking habits of the Scottish public.

THE NATIONAL REVIEW OF RESOURCE ALLOCATION FOR THE NHS IN SCOTLAND

The new formula for distribution:

Funds are allocated after considering

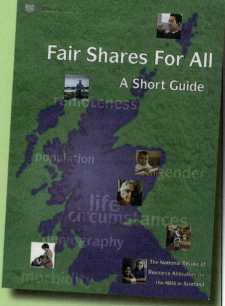

a) The size of each Health Board's population.

b) An adjustment to account for the profile of each Board's population in terms of age and sex.

c) An adjustment to reflect the needs arising from ill health (morbidity) and life circumstances (such as deprivation, poverty and ethnicity).

d) An adjustment to reflect the unavoidable excess cost of delivering health care in rural and remote areas of Scotland.

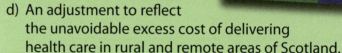

" Eighteen months ago I was asked to work out a fairer way of sharing more than £4 billion on the Health Service in Scotland. Sam Galbraith, then Scottish Minister for Health, wanted a new system which would replace the twenty-year-old SHARE formula—and give Scotland a lead in the UK in ending inequalities in health provision.

The new formula seeks to do three things.

● First to recognise and account for the links between deprivation and ill health which exist in our least advantaged communities. The review looked at the different life circumstances of communities across Scotland, examining, in particular, the connections between use of health services and factors such as unemployment, dependency on benefits, poor housing and early death rates. This analysis showed that there were significant links between such things as markers of deprivation, mortality and poverty, and the need for health services.

● Second, to account for the extra costs of delivering health services in rural and remote areas. Scotland has a unique rural geography which poses special challenges for the delivery of health care. Providing acute care for the citizens of Lerwick, living hundreds of miles across water from the nearest acute hospital, is a good deal more costly than providing acute services in Lanarkshire.

Equity of access to care should mean equity for all citizens wherever they live. Geography must no longer be an excuse for the gaps in health care which can occur for those living in remote and rural communities.

Those living in remote areas should have the reassurance that their local services are funded in a way that gives them the same opportunity of access to services as those living at either end of the M8.

● Third, to address the issue of inequalities in health care. We have established that there are those in society who, for reasons of social exclusion, do not access health services as effectively as others. We have posed a vital question: how should the allocation of resources address this difficult but crucial issue? "

Smoking Ban in Scotland

It is hoped that the smoking ban in enclosed public places (pubs, restaurants and other public places) introduced in Scotland on 26 March 2006 will dramatically reduce health inequalities in Scotland. First Minister, Jack McConnell stated:

> "Scotland will be proud that it has gone smoke-free ahead of any other part of the United Kingdom. In years ahead, people will look back on today as the day that Scotland took the largest single step to improve its health for generations."

Scotland has one of the worst health records in Europe with tobacco being a major contributor to ill health and premature death. It is hoped that the ban will act as an incentive for many to quit their smoking habit. It is estimated that the ban could save 600 lives every year and save the NHS £8 million annually. Lung cancer rates are 49% higher in Scotland than in England and Wales (see page 81) and it is clear that advertising campaigns against smoking have had limited impact.

The Scottish Executive cites figures to show that cigarette sales fell by 13% after a ban was introduced in 2003 in New York and by 16% in Ireland in 2004. The British Medical Association (BMA) claims that passive smoking kills 1,000 people a year in the United Kingdom and so the entire population will benefit from a ban. Not everyone supported the ban. Neil Rafferty of the pro-smoking lobby group, Forest, said, "Scotland is less free than it

was last week. Politicians now have a licence to intrude into our private lives."

The law which bans smoking in enclosed places in Scotland includes provision to raise the legal age for buying cigarettes to 18 if Ministers choose and this action is being considered by the Scottish Executive. In September 2006, Asda, the food retailer, raised the age at which it would allow customers to buy cigarettes to 18 in all of its 302 stores.

Some Health Boards are encouraging pregnant women to stop smoking by offering cash incentives. Women who give up smoking during pregnancy will be given £50 a month. NHS Tayside is spending £100,000 a year on "the reward

plus social support scheme". It is available for up to three months after childbirth if the mother remains smoke free. Almost 50% of pregnant women in deprived areas of Tayside smoke during pregnancy. As well as financial incentives pregnant smokers are being offered nicotine replacement therapy and professional support.

Smoking Ban in England

The UK Cabinet had been divided over whether to introduce a partial or blanket ban on smoking in public places. However, under pressure from anti-smoking campaigners, the 2006 Health Bill included legislative provisions to make virtually all enclosed public places and workplaces smoke free by summer 2007.

Do health campaigns work?

Part of the present strategy to improve health is for the government to spend millions of pounds on television, radio and newspaper campaigns. There is an ongoing debate over how effective at changing people's eating and drinking habits these promotions are.

In 2004 Health Scotland, formerly known as the Health Education Board for Scotland (HEBS), carried out fifty awareness events such as Bug Busting Day and National Smile Week. According to critics these had little impact. Research suggests that those who listen to the advice have already taken action to improve their lifestyles. In contrast, those who ignore or claim to be unaware of the numerous health messages are those who have the greatest need to change their way of life.

British artist David Hockney, who is pro-smoking, is opposed by an anti-tobacco protester during the 2005 Labour Party Conference.

Local Initiatives to tackle Health Inequalities—Have a Heart Paisley

Have a Heart Paisley aims to reduce heart disease and promote healthier, longer lives for the people of Paisley.

Launched in October 2000 as one of the Scottish Executive's four national health demonstration projects, *Have a Heart Paisley* has now entered a second phase of activities. Applying lessons learned from previous activities, the project is delivering a programme of work aimed at those most at risk of developing heart problems. With its partners in the community, the NHS and the local authority, *Have a Heart Paisley* aims to demonstrate through these programmes the degree to which preventive measures can improve heart health by tackling risk factors and unmet treatment needs.

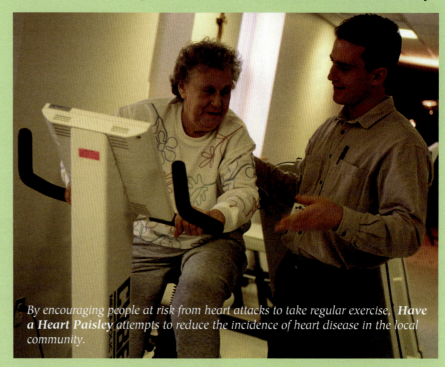

By encouraging people at risk from heart attacks to take regular exercise, **Have a Heart Paisley** *attempts to reduce the incidence of heart disease in the local community.*

Emerging lessons from the work of Have a Heart Paisley are also helping to guide future policy and practice in the prevention and treatment of heart disease throughout Scotland. The Heart Health Learning Network plays a key role in the dissemination of these lessons throughout the country.

The initiative has now entered its second phase. In phase two the demonstration project will work with its partners to deliver a targeted programme for the working age population and those with coronary heart disease in Paisley. *Have a Heart Paisley* Project Manager Cath Krawczyk said: "The project will now focus on preventing the development of heart disease amongst the working age people of Paisley."

Diet and Obesity

The strategy outlined in *Working Together for a Healthier Scotland* was influenced by the James Report. In 1998 the Labour government commissioned a committee of experts, under the chairmanship of Professor Philip James, to investigate how to stop children eating junk food. This is rich in sugar, fat and salt, all of which are linked to obesity and heart disease in later life. The main proposal was:

● to stop the sale of sweets, salty snacks and soft drinks inside schools;

● to curb junk food outlets near schools;

● to set a legal limit on the age at which children are allowed out of school during lunch-time; and

● to prohibit food companies targeting food advertising at the young.

For adults, numerous health promotion campaigns have been financed by the government to raise health awareness. Advertising on television and radio has had some impact. Many adults are now aware that they should try to eat five portions of fruit/vegetables a day and to reduce their salt intake. Campaigns to encourage improved physical fitness, such as 'Be All You Can Be' can be measured in part by the increase in the number of women out jogging and participating in special events.

The idea of Health Promoting Schools and the strategies to change the eating habits of young people are long-term policies which are difficult to measure at present.

(See Hungry for Success on page 91.) The TV chef Jamie Oliver's high profile campaign to improve school dinners was one factor in influencing government action in England, the cost of which was £220 million. In September 2006 the Labour government implemented new food standards in England and Wales, (see page 92) following the lead set by the Scottish Executive.

A 2006 review of the Hungry for Success programme provides some encouraging news, especially in primary schools. Peter Peacock, the Education Minister, accepted that it could take many years to ensure children developed lifelong healthy eating habits. He stated, "we have always known that bringing about such huge changes in the eating habits of the nation would not happen overnight, but could require sustained effort."

Critics of Health Promoting Schools argue that it has had little impact in secondary schools. They cite the fact that the number of pupils eating school meals in secondary schools has fallen to its lowest level since records began in 1999. Following the introduction of the new menus, take-up fell from 50.6% in 2002 to 46.1% in 2005. Take-up in England and Wales also fell (from 51% to 39%). Secondary pupils can leave school at lunchtime and may buy fatty food and fizzy drinks. Professor Annie Anderson, Professor of Health Nutrition at Dundee University, argues that: "Teenagers are the most challenging group to cater for. It is easy when they are little because they eat in schools, but there is such a diversity of competition in secondary with takeaways and vans because pupils can leave the school."

The Child Poverty Action Group is campaigning for free school meals to be introduced to ensure all pupils eat healthy school lunches. A bill put forward by the Scottish Socialist Party to introduce free school meals was unsuccessful.

The Scottish Executive is now considering banning the sale and availability of 'junk' food such as sweets and fizzy drinks on school premises. It will also monitor the extent to which all local authority schools have become health promoting.

At the UK level, attempts have been made to introduce a clampdown on television adverts for junk food to reduce obesity among children. Ofcom, the television regulator has refused to consider banning all unhealthy food adverts before the 9pm watershed. Ofcom proposals for curbing food adverts will focus on how specific products are promoted rather than the brand name. This means that organisations such as McDonalds will still be able to advertise the brand name McDonalds while avoiding reference to any of their unhealthy food products.

The celebrity chef Jamie Oliver wore a special suit to illustrate the effect of junk food on weight control. He campaigned for healthy diets through school meals.

HUNGRY FOR SUCCESS 2002–2006 Health Initiative

In November 2002, the Scottish Executive launched its £63.5 million initiative to get school children to switch from junk food to healthy eating—"from stodge to salads." The campaign introduced nutritional standards for school meals in primary and secondary schools. Food or drinks with a high sugar or salt content were to be phased out, and fresh fruit, vegetables and water were to become recommended food and drink.

In 2004, the Scottish Health Promoting Schools Unit produced the framework document *Being Well–Doing Well* which provides young people "with the confidence, skills, knowledge and resilience they will need to make healthier lifestyle choices".

Pupils and schools are supported by the National Health Promoting Schools website. By 2006 all primary schools were expected to have a Health Promotion Strategy with secondary schools having until 2007 to achieve this target.

Glasgow secondary schools have seen an increase in pupils choosing school meals with the introduction of Breakfast Clubs and Fuel Zone award schemes which allow pupils to accumulate points for eating a balanced, healthy diet. These points can be exchanged for rewards such as cinema tickets and iPods.

TACKLING CHILD OBESITY IN ENGLAND

School lunch rules from September 2006

☛ At least two portions of fruit and vegetables per day, per child, one of which should be salad or vegetables and one fruit—fresh, tinned or a fruit salad must be provided. A fruit-based dessert must be available at least twice a week in primaries.

☛ A non-dairy source of protein—meat, fish, eggs, nuts, pulses or non-green beans—must be available daily. Red meat must be available at least twice a week in primaries and three times in secondaries. Fish must be on offer once a week in primaries and twice in secondaries.

☛ Manufactured meat must meet legal minimum meat content levels. Economy burgers must not be used.

☛ A starchy food—bread, pasta, noodles, rice, potatoes, sweet potatoes, yams, millet, cornmeal—must be available daily.

☛ Fat or oil must not be used to cook starchy food more than three days a week.

☛ No more than two deep-fried items should be served per week.

☛ A dairy food must be available daily.

☛ All drinks are prohibited except skimmed or semi-skimmed milk, pure fruit juices, yoghurt and milk drinks with less than 5% added sugar, combinations of the above, low calorie hot chocolate, tea and coffee.

☛ No table salt is allowed.

☛ No confectionary or savoury snacks may be sold.

Other school food rules to be introduced in September 2006, to become law in September 2007

☛ No confectionary.

☛ No bagged savoury snacks. Nuts and seeds should be without added salt or sugar.

☛ A variety of fruit and vegetables should be available in all school food outlets.

☛ Pupils must have access to free, fresh drinking water at all times. This should be chilled.

☛ The only other drinks available will be skimmed or semi-skimmed milk, pure fruit juices, yoghurt and milk drinks.

One of the targets is to halt the rise in obesity among children under 16 by 2010. (It is estimated that child obesity has doubled over the last decade.) Schools will be urged to provide two hours of PE a week to complement the healthy diet regime. From 2007, every 4-year-old and 11-year-old will be weighed as part of the drive to curb obesity. Health authorities in England will be responsible for gathering evidence to give the government a detailed national picture of the obesity crisis.

Tackling Alcohol Abuse

A 2006 Health Report from the Scottish Executive stated that the strategies and targets set in *Working Together for a Healthier Scotland* had been successful in many areas. The death rates from heart disease and strokes had decreased, as had the number of strokes and also teenage pregnancy rates. However, it identified that targets set for obesity, diabetes and alcohol consumption had failed. As indicated on page 81, the Glasgow Centre for Population Health (GCPH) argues that if drastic measures are not taken then alcohol-related deaths in the Greater Glasgow area will double over the next two decades. The Registrar General's review of July 2006 revealed that 492 women died from alcohol-related diseases in 2005 compared with 224 in 1980.

The Scottish Executive's targets to cut underage drinking and excessive alcohol consumption among adults have not been reached, and in fact the Executive admits that the figures for both are worsening. This is a UK-wide not just a Scottish problem and is an indictment of Britain's drinking culture. (See Table 8.1.) Critics state that government action has encouraged this 'booze culture'. Recent licensing laws have removed the barrier to round-the-clock drinking and alcohol is now much more affordable to drink.

The critics argue that there should be a national debate on how to end Scotland and the UK's 'bevy culture'. The public needs to be educated to regard the abuse of alcohol in the same way as smoking—as antisocial, and harmful to the individual's health and to that of his/her family. A special tax should be placed on alcohol to discourage over-consumption (a strategy used in Scandinavian countries) and a review of licensing laws should be undertaken.

A UK initiative being considered is to place health warnings on alcohol and in places where it is sold. A spokesperson for the Scottish Executive stated that "a major cultural shift is required to change Scotland's long-standing drinking policies and this will require a concerted effort by a range of bodies including the drinks industry and the licensed trade".

The Scottish Executive is considering a report which recommends banning advertising alcohol on football and rugby players' shirts and a ban on children's leisurewear which displays drinks logos. At present football clubs such as Celtic and Rangers have lucrative sponsorship deals with drinks firms.

Mortality rates for liver cirrhosis 1997–2001 compared to those for 1987–91 (100 equals no change)		
	Men	**Women**
Scotland	204	146
England & Wales	169	144
Sweden	98	91
Norway	93	110
France	88	77
Portugal	66	66
Netherlands	103	112
Denmark	122	121
Ireland	143	123

Table 8.1

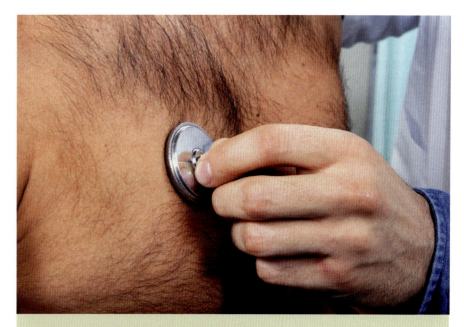

MEN'S HEALTH CLINICS

One problem associated with innovative health projects funded by the Scottish Executive is that when the money dries up the NHS authorities cannot afford to fund them. Such is the fate of men's health clinics.

Every NHS authority funds well woman clinics and in 2002 the Scottish Executive allocated £4 million to run 'well man' health clinics in areas of poor health. The clinics were set up as a result of concern about the lack of interest Scottish men take in their own well-being. (See health statistics below.) Ian Anderson, who attended one of the first pilot clinics in Falkirk, claims it changed his life. He has changed his eating and exercise habits and has lost a quarter of his body weight.

It is clear that the clinics have been very successful. An analysis of the first group of men who attended the Falkirk clinic revealed that over 50% had an undiagnosed health problem with nurses' tests picking up cancers, diabetes, heart disease and hypertension.

In June 2006 NHS Greater Glasgow and NHS Lothian stated that their "well man health clinics would close." One worker for NHS Greater Glasgow stated: "I am outraged they have withdrawn funding. Men's health in parts of Glasgow is pretty chronic. Imagine if they said they were going to withdraw well woman services. But they withdraw them from men and there's not a peep about it."

In Scotland
- ❖ 62% of men are overweight or obese
- ❖ 33% of men drink more than the recommended weekly limit
- ❖ 32% of men smoke
- ❖ 38% take regular exercise
- ❖ men aged between 15 and 64 attend their GP practice half as often as women
- ❖ suicides among men have increased by 75% since the early 1970s
- ❖ the heart disease death rate among men is the highest in the UK at 221 per 100,000
- ❖ lung cancer killed more than 2,000 men in 2004, the highest death rate in the UK

Chapter 9

The role of the private sector

The role of the private sector in providing health care and in working in partnership with the NHS to tackle health inequalities creates great controversy. On the one hand, opponents of the private sector claim that such partnerships will destroy state-funded health care provision and this 'creeping privatisation' will eventually create a USA-style model of a first-class private sector and a third-rate state system dealing with trauma and acute illness. Supporters of the involvement of the private sector argue that partnership models will reduce waiting lists, improve efficiency and provide state-of-the-art hospitals. The UK Labour government, once hostile to private health care, has now embraced working with the private sector. (The Scottish Executive finally followed suit in 2005.)

PRIVATE HEALTH CARE

In 2005 roughly 14% of the UK population was covered by private health insurance. A 2003 report from Laing and Buisson, *Private Health Analysis*, highlighted the significant increase in the number of Scots taking out private health cover. According to their figures 405,000 people now have medical insurance, equivalent to 8% of the population. Essential Healthcare, an online private health insurance company, stated: "Before now the typical person getting private care was a wealthy professional in their forties. Now there are far more young couples in their twenties and thirties."

WHAT IS PRIVATISATION?

The term privatisation covers a number of quite different practices within the area of health care.

+ The practice of patients 'going private' and paying for the services of GPs, hospital doctors or hospital provision.
+ The practice of the public sector buying services from the private sector: for example the hiring of medical equipment, or operations being provided by private hospitals.
+ The practice of contracting services out to the private sector (competitive tendering): for example ancillary services, namely laundry, cleaning, catering etc. being provided by a private firm.

The most recent practice of hospitals being built and run by private firms—Public Private Partnership Programmes (PPPP), originally known as Private Finance Initiatives (PFI)—have aroused great controversy.

About 90% of private patients in the UK pay their bills through private medical insurance schemes. It is estimated that of the seven million people covered by private medical insurance, four million have it as part of their employment package and so their employers meet the costs. The growth in private insurance has continued despite the Labour government ending tax relief on private medical insurance in 1997.

THE PROVIDERS

The private health insurance market is dominated by two Provident Associations, BUPA (British United Provident Association) and PPP (Private Patients Plan) who between them have almost 75% of the market share. Other major providers are Norwich Union and Standard Life.

Customers can choose from a wide range of health packages. These packages can be broadly classified into three categories—top of the range, standard and budget policies. Top of the range plans give full cover for treatment in most or all private hospitals and usually include extras such as home nursing. Standard policies cover a limited range of hospitals and have fewer extras. Budget plans offer an even narrower range of hospitals and often cover a limited range of illnesses.

The cost of insurance is high and increases as a person gets older which creates problems for the elderly. A top o the range plan with no restrictions can cost a 40-year-old £1,700 a year.

Disparities in cover

There are wide variations in terms of the age, social class and regional location of those individuals who have private health insurance.

+ The cost of health insurance increases significantly the older a person gets and this is now even higher with the ending of tax relief on health insurance for the over-60s. A further difficulty is that when people retire they lose any benefits they might have had from discounts through their employer's group scheme. Not surprisingly, therefore, the proportion of the 65–75 age group covered by health insurance is about half that of those aged under 65.

+ Partly as a consequence of the high cost of health insurance and the growing importance of company-paid schemes, the majority of customers enjoying such cover come from high income groups. The most recent statistics show that while 27% of professionals and 23% of employers / managers had some medical insurance cover, this compared with only 2% for the semi-skilled and 1% for the unskilled groups.

+ The General Household Survey showed that there were also large regional variations. The south-east of England had the highest coverage (parts of Buckinghamshire had rates in excess of 20%) and the north of the country the least (Scotland had only about 8%). This may, in part, reflect the higher standard of living and greater concentration of private health care facilities in the south-east of England.

THE COST OF COMMON OPERATIONS

Heart by pass	£12,500 – £15,500
Knee replacement	£7,500 – £9,500
Hip replacement	£7,000 – £9,500
Hysterectomy	£2,600 – £4,500
Hernia	£1,800 – £2,400

EXCLUSIONS ON MOST HEALTH POLICIES

X   All ailments known to exist before starting the policy

X   Services of a GP, dentist or optician

X   Health checks

X   Long-term hospital or nursing care

X   Transplants

X   Treatment on a kidney machine

X   Fertility treatment

X   Pregnancy and childbirth except, in some cases, when there are complications

X   Vasectomy and sterilisation

X   Abortion, unless medically necessary

X   HIV and AIDS-related conditions

X   Cosmetic surgery, unless necessary after an accident

X   Suicide attempts and resulting injuries

X   Illnesses caused by alcohol or drug abuse

X   Homeopathic or other alternative medicine

X   Appliances such as wheelchairs

X   Any treatment not referred by a GP

All private schemes, even the top of the range ones, contain certain exemptions. Costs vary enormously between the three categories of plan. Costs also vary depending upon age. A couple in their early fifties pay about £72 per month for a Norwich Union health care policy. On the other hand, a budget Legal and General Plan will insure someone between the ages of 18 and 24 for £9.99 per month.

THE PUBLIC v PRIVATE HEALTH CARE DEBATE

ARGUMENTS AGAINST PRIVATE HEALTH CARE

1 In the NHS all patients should be treated equally and according to need. Private medicine, on the other hand, is based on the ability to pay. It has created a two-tier health system—one (private medicine) for the well-off who seek care for acute conditions, and one (NHS) for the poor and the chronically and seriously ill.

2 When people choose to go private they are, effectively, queue jumping. Private hospitals deal with the easy work, leaving the difficult and expensive complaints to the NHS.

3 The majority of nurses working in the private sector were trained in the NHS at public expense. Moreover, many of them have special skills, such as intensive care and operating theatre skills, which are in short supply in the NHS.

4 Evidence suggests that some consultants who work for both sectors tend to neglect their public patients and favour their private ones. Private work interferes with NHS efficiency.

5 Most private hospitals do not have on-site emergency facilities, and if a crisis develops private patients have to be treated by the NHS.

6 Private patients often find that the cost of their treatment is far higher than they had been led to believe.

7 Many private patients are articulate and influential members of society. If they used the NHS for routine treatment, they would be unlikely to accept low standards or long waiting lists, and they would insist on improvements to the service.

ARGUMENTS FOR PRIVATE HEALTH CARE

1 Private treatment is not a luxury which only rich people can afford. Patients in the independent sector now represent a cross section of society through group insurance schemes. For example, union deals have brought firefighters and police officers into private health group insurance schemes.

2 Pressure is taken away from the NHS when people turn to private medicine. The NHS receives much-needed additional income from private patients who use pay beds.

3 A number of private hospitals offer courses in basic nurse training and post-qualification specialist training. This can also benefit the NHS as these nurses can leave the private sector at any time to work for the NHS.

4 Private practice enables hospital consultants to receive earnings similar to those they could gain abroad. This helps to stop a 'brain drain' of our hospital consultants.

5 Private hospitals and insurance companies have donated pieces of equipment to NHS hospitals, to be used by both public and private patients.

6 Some types of treatment, for example cosmetic surgery, are only available in the private sector.

7 Private patients still contribute to the running of the NHS through their compulsory National Insurance contributions. When people spend their money on private medicine they are helping to add to the total amount of resources spent on health care.

Has your little boy got private tonsils or public ones?

PRIVATE HOSPITALS

In the UK there are 220 private acute hospitals, 70 mental health hospitals and 1,500 nursing and residential care homes. Private health care provided an estimated £18 million worth of health services in 2003. Scotland has eight private hospitals with a total of over 900 beds available for private patients. In 2002 the HCI private hospital in Clydebank was purchased for £37.5 million by the Scottish Executive to help reduce waiting times for treatment and was renamed the Golden Jubilee National Hospital.

In December 2001, Labour ended its historical ideological opposition to private medicine when the government signed a deal with BUPA to carry out operations on NHS patients. This decision was based on an urgent need to reduce waiting lists and this has been achieved in England and Wales.

The Scottish Executive was less enthusiastic about embracing the private sector and this delay partly explains the failure to reduce waiting times in Scotland. In April 2005, First Minister Jack McCon-

nell admitted that hospital waiting targets were twice as long as they were in England. The UK Labour Manifesto for the 2005 general election stated that waiting times would be reduced to eighteen weeks. In contrast the Scottish Labour Manifesto said thirty six weeks. The SNP's election campaign poster of a skeleton in a wheelchair with the slogan "How much longer must patients wait?", displayed Labour's vulnerability over health issues.

The failure to reduce waiting lists explains the number of Scots 'going private'. Over 7,400 patients out of 34,000 who were admitted for day patient treatment at Scotland's private hospitals paid from their own pocket.

The January 2006 NHS Scotland reforms introduced by Andy Kerr, the Scottish Health Minister, included a key role for the private sector. Following the English model, contracts were signed with the private sector using existing facilities to offer patients evening and weekend appointments. Unused wards, especially in the Golden Jubilee, will be leased to the private sector. The private mobile services much used in England will be located where they are most needed. Mr Kerr stated: "If reducing waiting times means using private sector facilities it really doesn't matter so long as the patients are getting the right service."

Critics of this expansion of the private sector using public funding are concerned about the loss of highly trained staff to the private sector. They are concerned that funds will be diverted from the NHS to the private sector (and its shareholders.) A further concern is that the NHS will have to step in if private treatment fails. In May 2006, fourteen patients were admitted to hospital with serious infections after eye surgery to remove cataracts at a private clinic had gone wrong.

The private sector also plays a crucial role in providing residential care for the elderly. In May 2006, Highland Council agreed to put a number of the care homes run by the local authority out to private tender. The Council stated that it did not have the funds to refurbish the properties and it hoped to privatise six of its twenty care homes.

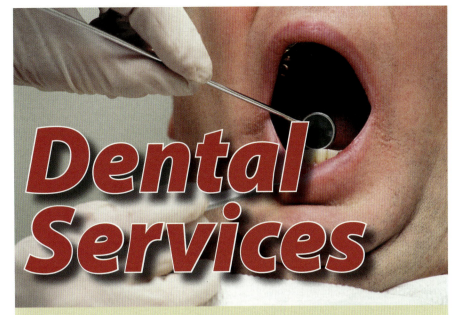

Dental Services

This primary care service has experienced privatisation in terms of delivery. Many dentists across the UK have left the NHS and will only treat private patients. This trend has accelerated in recent years with 43,000 Scottish adults losing their NHS dentist in 2005 alone. The 2006 figures make depressing reading with only 47% of Scottish adults being registered with an NHS dentist. In NHS Highland the figure is only 25%.

The Scottish Executive Dental Improvement Plan promises to recruit 200 extra dentists by 2008 by increasing the number of students studying dentistry and by recruiting dentists from Eastern Europe. A sliding scale of payments to reward increased NHS work has been introduced.

The crisis in Scottish dentistry is reflected in the poor oral hygiene of Scottish children who have the worst teeth in Britain. An April 2006 study into the dental health of 11-year-olds revealed that Scottish children are slipping behind those in England and Wales. While the proportion of children with decayed, missing, or filled teeth has fallen by 40% in England, over the same period, Scotland has achieved only a 30% reduction in the thousands of children who require restorative dental treatment. In Scotland only 46% are receiving dental treatment compared with almost 60% in 1999. Co-author of the study Zoe Nugent stated: "We need to introduce a mobile dental service to visit the areas of deprivation."

The Scottish Executive stands by its targets of ensuring that 60% of 11- to 12-year-olds are free of tooth decay by 2010. Part of the problem is that Scottish children consume more sweets and fizzy drinks than their English counterparts and it is hoped that the reform of school meals will reduce tooth decay. (See page 91 – 92.)

Private Sector – NHS Scotland Contracts 2006

- ❖ annual £15 million contract to be made with private sector
- ❖ 1,000 orthopaedic patients to be treated at Ross Hall private hospital
- ❖ 1,000 patients in NHS Tayside with ear nose and throat problems to be treated by private firms

COMPETITIVE TENDERING

In 1983 (1987 in Scotland), Margaret Thatcher's Conservative government introduced compulsory competitive tendering for catering, domestic and laundry services in the NHS (sometimes referred to as ancillary services). Under this process the in-house NHS workforce competes for the contract with the private sector. The Conservatives regarded competitive tendering as an opportunity to improve the efficiency of the public sector and to encourage private enterprise. The highest cost in a 24-hour service, which the NHS requires, is staff and so private contractors tend to cut wages and conditions and reduce staffing levels. In 1986 there were 67,000 full-time domestic workers in the NHS. Twenty years on the figure has almost halved with only 36,000 domestic workers employed.

While the NHS has made savings, it has been at the cost of cleanliness. It is no coincidence that as standards have fallen there has been an increase in MRSA infections. An Audit Scotland 2003 Report made depressing reading. It identified twenty hospitals as giving cause for concern in terms of poor levels of cleanliness in wards. Only half of Scotland's hospitals have high levels of cleanliness in their wards. The low wages paid to staff led to high levels of staff vacancies and staff turnover. High levels of absence through sickness reflected low morale. Some hospitals, such as the Victoria Royal Infirmary in Glasgow, have improved cleanliness by bringing their cleaning services back in-house. The PPPP Hairmyres Hospital received the lowest category, 4. The inspectors stated that "under the terms of the contract the external private contractor did not have to explain why it had failed to reach acceptable levels".

The new PPPP hospital to be built in Larbert (see page 100) will use a private firm to provide catering,

Working conditions of ancillary workers like catering staff were often reduced by competitive tendering.

cleaning, porters and other domestic services within the hospital. Steve Hamill, Unison's assistant branch secretary, condemned this decision. He stated: "our staff who have won national awards for catering and cleaning standards in 2005 are now being sold off to the private sector."

PUBLIC PRIVATE PARTNERSHIPS

The Conservative government introduced the Private Finance Initiative (PFI) in 1992. [Labour retained the policy and changed the name to Public Private Partnership Programme (PPPP)]. Under this initiative a private consortium designs, builds and operates developments such as schools and hospitals which require to be paid back over an agreed period of time. In effect, the local NHS Trust pays an annual fee to the consortium for the use of the hospital which covers the rent of the building, the cost of support services and, of course, construction costs.

The Labour Party, while in opposition, claimed that PFI projects would endanger the NHS, that health service workers would lose

their employment rights and that privatisation of the NHS would be the logical outcome of the PFI.

When Labour came to power in 1997, it announced that it would continue the Private Finance Initiative to enable the NHS to be modernised. "We cannot build an NHS for the twenty first century with hospitals built in the nineteenth century," declared Alan Millburn, the then Labour Health Minister.

The appeal of the scheme is that the Treasury does not have to borrow the money and hand it over to the NHS. In the short-term the government and taxpayers benefit. The private consortium raises the money which is paid back by the NHS Trust (and the taxpayer) over a thirty five-year period.

PPPP became an issue during the May 1999 elections for the Scottish Parliament and there was strong opposition from within the Scottish trade unions. Aware of the depth of criticism against PPPP, in June 1999 the government announced important changes to PPPP contracts.

Significantly these concessions, which apply throughout the UK, were announced first to the Scottish Parliament by the then Scottish Finance Minister, Jack McConnell. The new terms were as follows;

1   Most facilities built under PFI/PPPP can return to public ownership at the end of their contract period.

2   In future, surplus land will not be included in such projects unless it represents value for money to the taxpayer.

3   Staff transferred to the private sector will retain the wages and working conditions which they held as hospital porters, cleaners, catering staff or in other ancillary posts. This will include their pension rights.

PFI/PPPP
THE DEBATE

Arguments for

1   Public Private Partnership Programmes (PPPP) are different from PFI. As the new title suggests, the emphasis is on partnership and a close relationship between the interests of the public and private enterprise.* The changes made in June 1997 to protect the rights of ancillary workers further distance PPPP from PFI.
    * Clinical services, which were part of the Conservative PFI, are not included in PPPP.

2   It offers the best value for taxpayers' money and provides state-of-the-art hospitals. As former Health Minister Sam Galbraith said, "I am fed up going to hospitals and seeing fabric that is unacceptable. I am going to do what is correct for patients and use the best and quickest method of delivery that benefits patients."
    All over Britain brand new hospitals will be built to replace Victorian buildings. By 2006, fifteen of these hospitals were open, offering a twenty first century hospital experience.

3   The Labour Party claims that it is not breaking its 1997 electoral pledges. The manifesto stated, "We must put together the best combination of public and private finance to review infrastructure." Under PPPP, a new hospital will be built over a four-year period, whereas it would take from eight to ten years to build it with public funds. PPPP hospitals are being built on time and mostly within budget.

4   The reduction in the number of beds means that savings can be redirected to GPs and community care. This change in emphasis has not been brought about by PFI / PPPP but is a continuation of policies introduced in the 1980s to move from hospital treatment to a more cost-effective type of health care such as preventive visits from the district nurse and minor surgery by GPs.

Arguments against

1   PFI / PPPP is a Thatcher legacy and should be abandoned on ideological grounds. The changes made by Labour are minor and it was only through the opposition of the trade unions that the rights of ancillary workers are now protected.

2   PFI / PPPP is, in fact, costing far more than the traditional public funding of capital development. Allyson Pollack, a respected academic, claims that taxpayers will be charged more than 10% interest on the Edinburgh Royal Infirmary PFI, compared with 4.5% if the hospital borrowed directly. The British Medical Association (BMA) claims that the cost of the Edinburgh Royal Infirmary PFI hospital will be £720 million over twenty five years. If publicly financed it would be £180 million.

3   Many of the PFI / PPPP agreements are shrouded in commercial secrecy. Private companies are making decisions on the number of beds without consulting medical experts. There is a need for open decision making and greater accountability. The British Medical Association argues that money which should be used for patient care will leave the NHS as risk free private profit.

4   PFI reduces the number of beds available and, in the long run, will add to the length of waiting lists. New PFI hospitals built in Halifax, Norwich and Edinburgh have 30% fewer beds than the old buldings. This is a form of controlled expenditure and rationing; fewer patients means financial savings. Again the PFI hospitals are encouraged to increase the number of private patients they treat and this will further reduce the number of NHS patients.

THE PFI/PPPP INVESTMENT

Overall, sixty four hospitals will be funded through PPPP and, according to the government, without PPPP it would have taken thirty years to fund and build all of these new hospitals. At present, Scotland has three PPPP acute hospitals, Wishaw General, Edinburgh Royal Infirmary and Hairmyres, East Kilbride. In May 2006, the Scottish Executive announced plans for a £300 million PPPP super hospital to be built in Larbert. It will consist of a village of buildings and will provide 800 beds. This new hospital will replace Falkirk and Stirling Royal Infirmaries and this has created local opposition.

The PPPP scheme is still an area of controversy. The June 2006 decision to downgrade Monklands Hospital's Accident and Emergency Department rather than that of Hairmyres angered many groups. They argued that the Hairmyres department was retained because the private contractor would still have to be paid even if wards were empty.

A 2005 report into the development of the new Edinburgh Royal Infirmary uncovered a series of failures in its provision of services and financial management. There has also been a significant reduction in the number of acute beds in the new hospital. Dr Matthew Dunnigan, a retired consultant, stated

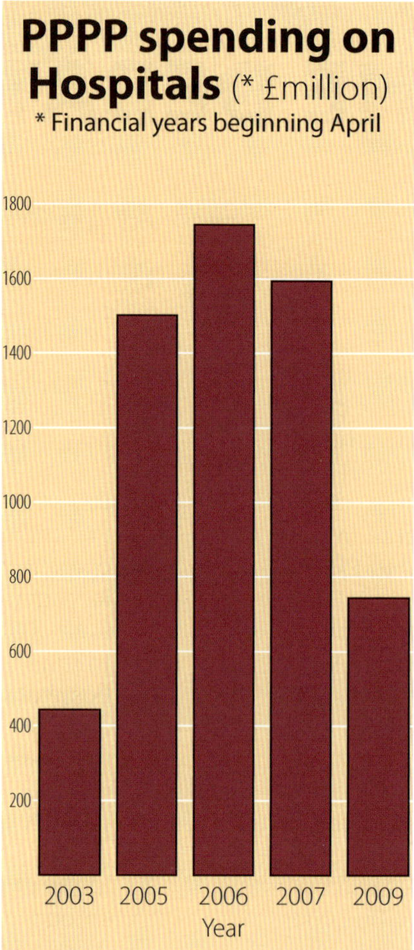

PPPP spending on Hospitals (* £million)
* Financial years beginning April

Figure 9.1 Source: Department of Health

that "for various reasons, Scotland enjoyed an advantage over England in the number of acute beds per head of population. But because of PPPP Lothian is being driven down to English levels."

Below are some further criticisms of PPPP schemes

☞ In a PPPP development in South London, changing a light bulb can cost £85 as the work has been sub-contracted and is costed on an hourly basis.

☞ In the same unit the change of use of a room had to be negotiated with another Trust: the process took nine months.

☞ A clause in one PPPP development in the south of England enabled the provider to increase the agreed cost from £35 million to £44 million once work had begun in 2005.

☞ A PPPP hospital which exceeded the number of operations specified in the contract had to pay the private consortium extra money.

☞ There are disputes in some PPPP hospitals where staff are required to accept worse terms and conditions of service than they had enjoyed within the NHS, despite assurances to the contrary. Significantly, a report by Health Facilities Scotland in August 2006 awarded Edinburgh Royal Infirmary the second lowest mark in the country for cleanliness.

Hairmyres hospital in South Lanarkshire was built as part of a PPPP.

Chapter 10

The debate over the provision of health care

This final chapter considers finance and demographic pressures, both key factors in any debate over the provision of health care. The chapter also provides an assessment of the NHS in the period 1997–2006.

FINANCING THE NHS

NHS income comes from three main sources and, as Figure 10.1 illustrates, general taxation provides the lion's share. The assumption made by Aneurin Bevan in 1948 that expenditure on health services would decline once the backlog of ill health had been tackled was quickly proved to be wrong. A consistent feature of the NHS has been the continuous growth in spending in real terms. In 1949 the service cost £437 million; by 1997 expenditure had risen to £44 billion. Over the same period, the real cost of the NHS increased fivefold. This explains why finance has always been

an issue within the NHS. The Wanless Report of 2001 concluded that a health service funded through taxation was the most efficient way of delivering care. The Labour government endorsed this approach and dismissed alternative models such as the system of social insurance used in France and Germany. (See below.)

In 2003 Gordon Brown, the Chancellor of the Exchequer, announced a massive boost in NHS spending for the period 2003–2008. (See Figures 10.2 and 10.3.) This would bring UK health spending as a percentage of GDP in line with European levels. In 1997–98 spending on the NHS in England was £34 billion; by 2007–08 the

figure will have risen to £90 billion. In 1997–98 spending on the NHS in Scotland was £4.7 billion; by 2007–08 the figure will have risen to £10.3 billion. Yet despite this massive increase the NHS in England and Wales faced a cash crisis in Spring 2006, while in Scotland, Argyll and Clyde Health Board ran up debts of £80 million in 2005.

The explanation for this apparent contradiction is that while government spending on the NHS rises faster than general inflation, the tendency is for the NHS to have a much higher rate of inflation than the economy as a whole. The NHS is a victim of its own success. The reasons for this are due to a combination of factors.

(Continued on page 103)

Paying for the NHS
1997/98

- **12%** national insurance
- **6%** charges
- **82%** general taxation

Figure 10.1

HEALTH CARE IN OTHER COUNTRIES

France
The French health care system is funded through tax revenues and social health insurance contributions from employers and employees. French patients have a free choice of doctors and hospitals.

Germany
The German system is funded through social health insurance contributions. Outpatient care is delivered by private, office-based doctors. Inpatient care is provided by a mix of public and private providers.

Netherlands
Dutch health care has three main elements: universal insurance for long-stay care and mental health, social health insurance for those on low incomes, and voluntary private health insurance for those on high incomes.

Paying for Health ...
THE OPTIONS

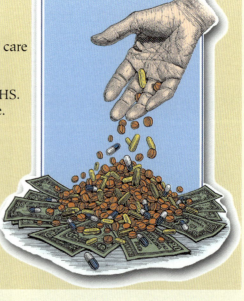

Raise taxes

Advantages: Easy to operate and allows swift access to funds. Opinion polls suggest that voters would favour an increase in taxation to provide greater funds for health and education.

Disadvantages: Politically risky. Historically the Labour Party has been regarded as a party of high taxation and views such a tag as a vote loser. Could also lead to inflation and could weaken the economy.

Levy a specific (hypothecated) health care tax

Advantages: Public would be able to see where their money is being spent, and may be less resistant to paying more. According to opinion polls, public are in favour of such a scheme. Revenue raised from smokers could, for example, be additional income awarded to the NHS.

Disadvantages: Additional costs of raising or administering the money may not result in proportionate benefits; could undermine willingness to find less popular spending. Politically a risky move.

Introduce compulsory state approved insurance (stakeholder health insurance)

Advantages: Provides general cover, yet gives consumers more indication of what they are paying for. Proposal could be extended to enable poorer people to have their premiums paid by the government.

Disadvantages: Problems for those who are not in employment and cannot afford health cover; an additional financial burden; could be regarded as an increase in taxation. If extended to all adults a 'means-test' system would have to be introduced.

Encourage more private health insurance

Advantages: People can choose to pay for what they want; adds to health care without increasing taxation.

Disadvantages: No access to treatment for the poor and those considered 'high risk'; administration can be expensive; may divert resources from NHS. Tax relief on medical insurance premiums will reduce government income.

Apply user charges

Advantages: Raises ready money—£5 per GP visit could raise £1 billion; £10 a day for hospital accommodation could raise £200 million.

Disadvantages: This would be unpopular with the public and would destroy the concept of a 'free' NHS. There would have to be exemptions for the young, the elderly and the poor and an expensive bureaucracy would have to be set up to administer the scheme. It would create discord in a hospital with those patients paying 'hotel charges' expecting preferential treatment and service.

Introduce special savings accounts

Advantages: Encourage people to make their own provision through savings in high interest 'health' accounts. Savings may build up into substantial sums for hospital treatment. Low interest loans to be made available for individuals to pay for immediate operations.

Disadvantages: Encourages the growth of the private sector and fails to address the needs of those on a low income. Would widen health inequalities, already a serious problem in Britain today.

The growing number of elderly people has profound implications for the NHS. Health costs for the over-75s, for example, are about seven times more than those for the population as a whole. Meeting the needs of the elderly has created a different approach between Scotland and England and is an area of concern for the British public. (See pages 104–105.)

The introduction of new wonder drugs which improve survival rates is one of the biggest cost pressures on health provision. The NHS drug bill is rising by around 13% each year and shows no sign of diminishing. Spending on Statins, a drug taken by 1.8 million people, costs £700 million a year. This drug has led to a dramatic fall in the number of patients needing cardiac surgery.

75% of the total NHS budget is spent on salaries. Much of the new money allocated to the NHS has gone on salaries. Centrally negotiated contracts for hospital consultants, family doctors and nurses have proved much dearer than expected. The funding allocated to finance the 'agenda for change' pay deal has not fully covered the extra cost and this explains why many hospitals and Health Boards are facing financial deficits. Consultants and doctors in the UK are now the highest paid in Europe. (See Audit Scotland Report.)

Audit Scotland Report July 2006

This report stated that the extra NHS cash is being used to pay inflated salaries to consultants and doctors. The cost of the settlement was four times greater than the original government estimate, yet according to Audit Scotland there was little evidence that it had improved patient care.

Scotland's 3,500 hospital consultants receive, on average, annual salaries of £94,000, a figure which excludes their private work. The new performance pay contract for Scotland's 4,000 GPs now means that some doctors are earning £100,000 a year. The report confirmed that Britain has the highest paid consultants and family doctors in Europe.

The situation in England is similar. Under the new 2004 contract GPs are able to opt out of having to provide out-of-hours care and many have done so. The responsibility for organising urgent care now lies with the 300 Primary Care Trusts (PCTs) which organise medical care outwith hospitals.

The Department of Health in England allocated £322 million to PCTs in 2005–06 to cover the cost of the new out-of-hours service. The National Audit Office (NAO) stated that the actual cost is likely to be £392 million, a shortfall of £70 million. The NAO criticised many PCTs for failing to meet quality requirements set by the government for the out-of-hours service. The Scottish equivalent, NHS 24, has also been heavily criticised.

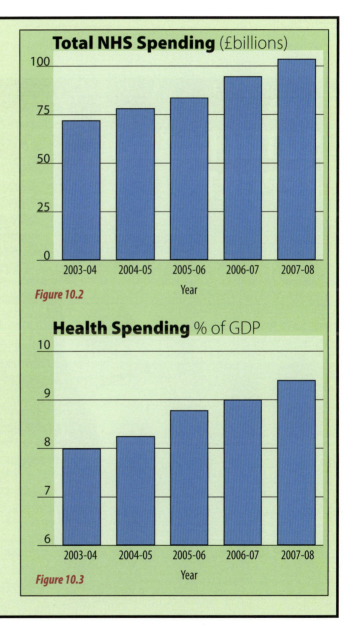

Total NHS Spending (£billions)

Figure 10.2

Health Spending % of GDP

Figure 10.3

THE ELDERLY

The elderly are a growing group within society and some critics argue that they suffer from health inequalities in terms of ageism within the NHS, and a failure to provide sufficient funding to care for their health needs. Numerous reports have highlighted the poor treatment that many elderly people receive in hospitals or care homes. A 2006 report by the Healthcare Commission Inspectorate stated that "the elderly are being neglected, treated poorly and marginalised in the health system".

The Sutherland Report of 1999 (see below) recommended that medical care in nursing and residential homes should be provided free and should not be means-tested. The UK government refused to implement its findings on the grounds of cost. In contrast the Scottish Executive introduced free personal care for the elderly and regards it as one of its flagship policies.

The situation in England is that pensioners living in care homes can receive social security payments (nursing care and attendance allowances) which are means-tested and paid from the UK social security budget. These funds are no longer available to Scottish recipients of personal care. This means that the cost of free personal care is totally paid by the Scottish taxpayer with the Scottish Executive no longer able to access the UK budget.

A June 2006 report by the Health Committee of the Scottish Parliament, while praising free personal care for the elderly, highlighted problems and made appropriate recommendations. (See page 105.) The Scottish Executive correctly states that its policy on the elderly maintains a cornerstone of the NHS founding principles, namely to provide a service free at the point of delivery regardless of income, whereas the English system is only free for the poor elderly.

the SUTHERLAND REPORT

In December 1997, the new Labour government set up a Royal Commission on the Long-Term Care of the Elderly under the Chairmanship of Sir Stewart Sutherland. In February 1999 it made its report and recommended that all health services should be provided free and that the threshold for contributing to the living and housing costs should be raised to savings of £60,000.

The Commission denied that there was a 'demographic time bomb' which would make long-term care unaffordable. It argued that the additional cost of its free-care proposals was only about £1 billion a year—although its suggestion that the state should also pay more to those who care for old people in their own homes would increase this total to £1.4 billion. Britain, the Report argued, was a wealthy country where the living standards of its citizens increased every decade. It could therefore afford the cost of providing dignity and security to its elderly citizens.

FREE PERSONAL CARE IN SCOTLAND

For people living in a care home

People aged 65 and over are entitled to an allowance of £145 a week for their personal care and a further £65 a week if they need nursing care. The local authority pays the money directly to the care home and individuals pays the difference between that and the weekly cost of living in the home if they have assets of more than £19,500 including the value of their homes.

For people receiving free personal care at home

People will be assessed by the local authority Social Work Department and a decision will be made on whether they need a care package. If they meet the criteria, they will receive the care free of charge. Support for non-personal care, such as meals on wheels, or help with housework, will be means-tested.

The report highlighted that the elderly were suffering from post code inequalities. Only eleven of the thirty two local councils did not have a waiting list of elderly people who were waiting to have their needs assessed. Over 4,000 pensioners fell into this category. The authorities with the biggest waiting lists were Dundee, North Ayrshire, and Argyll and Bute.

The Committee found inconsistencies between local authorities with some charging for food preparation while others provided this free. Renfrewshire Council apologised for employing a debt agency to chase up the debt of an Alzheimer's sufferer who had failed to pay for food preparation. It also discovered that some of the authorities had not used the money allocated by the Scottish Executive for free personal care but instead had used it for other services.

Report by the Scottish Parliament's Health Committee on free personal care for the elderly.

June 2006

The Committee praised the free care policy for improving services for the elderly, helping to reduce the problem of bed blocking in hospitals and allowing many people to be supported in their own homes.

In 2005 local authorities were given £153 million to pay for free personal care for the elderly. This figure will rise to £169 million for 2007–08.

Committee's recommendations

● a detailed Executive review of the finances of free care for the elderly

● an end to the legal loopholes that allow councils to 'ration' free care

● new guidlines to ensure that services such as food preparation are provided free

● Ministers should prevent councils from delaying assessments for financial reasons, either by backdating all claims or by enforcing a deadline for assessment

AN AGEING POPULATION

The population of the UK has grown steadily in recent years. (See Table 10.1.) In 2001 the UK population was 59.1 million, a figure which is projected to rise to 61.9 million by 2011. While the population of England will increase by 5% in this period, the Scottish population will remain static. In the same period the number of elderly people will increase at a faster rate. This increase in the number of elderly people in the population, linked to the decline in the birth rate, will dramatically increase the proportion of elderly people in UK society.

Table 10.4 illustrates that population ageing is a common characteristic across the European Union, a trend which is placing a strain on health provision across Europe. Italy has the largest percentage of people aged 65 and over, followed by Germany and Greece. Ireland has the lowest proportion at 11.1% and the highest number of under-15s (20.9%).

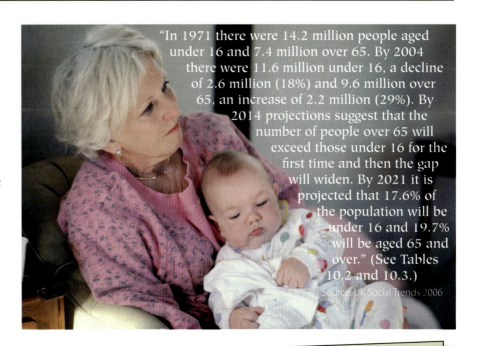

"In 1971 there were 14.2 million people aged under 16 and 7.4 million over 65. By 2004 there were 11.6 million under 16, a decline of 2.6 million (18%) and 9.6 million over 65, an increase of 2.2 million (29%). By 2014 projections suggest that the number of people over 65 will exceed those under 16 for the first time and then the gap will widen. By 2021 it is projected that 17.6% of the population will be under 16 and 19.7% will be aged 65 and over." (See Tables 10.2 and 10.3.)

Source: UK Social Trends 2006

Scotland's Demographic Time bomb

◆ Scotland's population is falling at a faster rate than anywhere else in Europe

◆ While the populations of England, Wales and Northern Ireland are predicted to rise, Scotland's will fall. It is predicted that Scotland's population will have fallen to 4.84 million by 2027

◆ By 2019, 35% of those over 65 will be suffering from dementia

It is estimated that while 15% of the English population will be over 65 by 2021, the figure in Scotland will be 25%.

Population of the United Kingdom
(Millions)

	1981	2001	2011	2021
UK	56.4	59.1	61.9	64.7
England	46.8	49.4	52.0	54.6
Wales	2.8	2.9	3.0	3.2
Scotland	5.2	5.1	5.1	5.0
N/ern Ireland	1.5	1.7	1.8	1.8

Table 10.1
Source: Social Trends 2006

Growth of Elderly in UK
(millions)

	65+	75+
1971	7.4	2.6
1991	9.0	4.0
2001	9.4	4.4
2011	10.4	4.9
2021	11.6	5.5

Table 10.3 Source: Social Trends 2006

Population by sex and age (selected age groups)

Males (000)

	under 16	65–74	75+	All Ages
1971	7,318	1,999	842	27,167
1991	5,976	2,272	1,358	27,412
2001	6,077	2,308	1,621	28,832
2011	5,744	2,652	2,068	30,438
2021	5,821	3,158	2,664	31,943

Females (000)

	under 16	65–74	75+	All Ages
1971	6,938	2,765	1,802	28,761
1991	5,709	2,795	2,634	29,530
2001	5,786	2,640	2,805	30,281
2011	5,487	2,898	2,931	31,454
2021	5,578	3,452	3,465	32,784

Table 10.2
Source: Social Trends 2006

Population: by age,
selected EU comparison 2004 (%)

	under 15	15–64	65 & over
Cyprus	20.0	68.1	11.9
Czech Republic	15.2	70.8	13.9
France	18.6	65.1	16.4
Germany	14.7	67.3	18.0
Greece	14.5	67.7	17.8
Ireland	20.9	68.0	11.1
Italy	14.2	66.6	19.2
Netherlands	18.5	67.6	13.8
Portugal	15.7	67.4	16.8
Spain	14.5	68.6	16.9
UK	18.2	65.8	16.0
EU average	16.4	67.2	16.5

Table 10.4 Source: Social Trends 2006

RATIONING HEALTH CARE

Lord Winton, a leading fertility expert and Labour peer, criticised the NHS and raised the issue of rationing which "unofficially exists within the NHS". Waiting lists, clinical decisions, approved drug lists and spending priorities are all mechanisms to manage limited resources. Choices have always been made about which patients should receive treatment and which should not.

Many people feel uneasy with the process of rationing due to the fact that decisions are being taken on an ad hoc basis by individual Primary Care Trusts (PCTs) in England and Wales and Health Boards in Scotland. Critics have pointed out that if the health service is to remain a national one, it is unacceptable that treatments are available in one area but not in the next. A recent example of this 'post code lottery' is the use of the drug herceptin in tackling the early stages of breast cancer. While some PCTs were prescribing herceptin others were refusing to prescribe it for patients on the grounds of cost. In 2006 Anne Marie Rodgers won her case against Swindon PCT, which was forced to pay for her herceptin treatment. The court ruled that it was "irrational for the trust to refuse to prescribe the drug when all other PCTs had such a policy."

In the UK, health authorities take guidance from the National Institute for Health and Clinical Excellence (NICE) in England and Wales and the Scottish Medicines Consortium (SMC) in Scotland. These bodies decide if new drugs are cost effective and if they should be offered to NHS patients. In 2006 SMC decided not to recommend Temozolomide (a breakthrough treatment in brain tumour therapy) as it declared the drug did not represent value for money. A full course of the treatment—which is marketed as Temodof—costs about £11,000. This decision was taken despite thirty six of Britain's leading cancer specialists writing to Patricia Hewitt, the Health Secretary at Westminster, and to the Scottish Executive asking that Temozolomide be freely available on prescription.

East Suffolk NHS Trust was heavily criticised in 2005 for proposing that obese people should not receive hip and knee replacements. The ban would apply to people with a Body

Mass Index (BMI) of 30. (This would be a woman who is 1.58 metres tall and weighs 75 kilos or a man who is 1.78 metres tall and weighs 93.8 kilos.)

AN ASSESSMENT OF THE NHS

'How successful has the NHS been?' A clear enough question perhaps, but one which is difficult to answer. The problem centres on what *criteria* should be used to measure its achievements. An obvious starting point might be to examine the NHS's record in terms of whether it has been able to satisfy the original assumptions and aims set by its creators.

Fixed quantity of illness?

Beveridge had argued in his report that there was a fixed quantity of illness in society and that setting up a national health service would enable the backlog of demand to be met. Once that had been achieved, there would be a gradual reduction in the incidence of ill health and the number of cases the NHS would have to treat would eventually stabilise at a much lower level. The reality, however, has been very different. Every measure of how much services are being used points to the same conclusion—the demands on the NHS have increased rapidly and consistently year after year.

With the benefit of hindsight, it is easy to see why Beveridge's assumption that there was a fixed quantity of illness was mistaken. The combined effects of medical progress and social change have meant that health problems have merely been transformed instead of being eliminated. Advances in medical treatment have greatly increased people's expectations of what medicine can do for them. People now expect treatment for conditions which in an earlier period would have been tolerated. While many infectious diseases have been largely brought under control, others have begun to replace them. The appearance of AIDS in the 1980s is a dramatic

THE HEALTH SERVICE AT 50

Throughout Britain in June 1998, special church services were held to commemorate the fiftieth anniversary of the National Health Service. It was fitting that the party which had introduced the NHS was once again in power when it was time to celebrate its achievements. The media—newspapers and television—reflected on a service which follows us from 'the cradle to the grave' and the impact the NHS has had on our daily lives. The consensus from the media was that the NHS had transformed the lives of the British people, but through its successes had created ever rising expectations and financial costs. As *The Economist* pointed out, "the more medical science achieves, the longer people live and the more they end up costing the NHS." Finance has been an issue since the creation of the NHS in 1948.

Almost ten years on the question of how successful the NHS has been is still being asked.

1948   1998

TOOTH DECAY

Toothbrushes are a fashion accessory and fluoride unknown. In working-class areas in the north of England many people have all their teeth extracted before they are 30 to save paying dentists' fees.

Tooth decay dramatically reduced by better diet, health education, fluoride toothpaste and fluoridation of some drinking water.

RADIOLOGY

Basic X-rays and early barium meals available. Medicine still largely a 'hands on' profession—looking, listening, touching and inspired guesswork.

Sophisticated diagnostic X-rays available; also ultrasound scans and nuclear isotope scanning to 'see' inside the body without surgery.

VACCINATIONS

Bed rest, fresh air and a change of diet are the only treatments available for many diseases. In 1945, diphtheria claimed 722 lives, whooping cough 689, measles 729 and TB 23,955.

Polio, TB, whooping cough, measles, mumps and rubella have all been virtually eliminated by mass childhood immunisation.

LIVER FAILURE

No treatment—patients are put on a diet and sent home to die.

Liver transplants save more than 700 lives a year.

HEART DISEASE

No treatment for heart failure and disease is usually fatal.

Heart transplants, coronary artery bypasses and pacemakers save thousands of lives and improve the quality of many others. In 1997, seventy two people received a new heart.

KIDNEY DISEASE

The reasons for kidney failure are not understood and patients are sent home to die.

Almost 14,000 people receive kidney dialysis. Nearly 400 people a year receive a kidney transplant.

HIGH BLOOD PRESSURE

Seriously ill patients with high blood pressure are put on a low salt diet of rice and water. For most there is no treatment and a risk of stroke or heart disease before they reach retirement.

One in ten of the population over 40 is receiving treatment for high blood pressure. Anti-hypertension drugs save thousands from stroke, heart disease, disability and possible death.

Source: Adapted from *The Observer*, 5.7.98

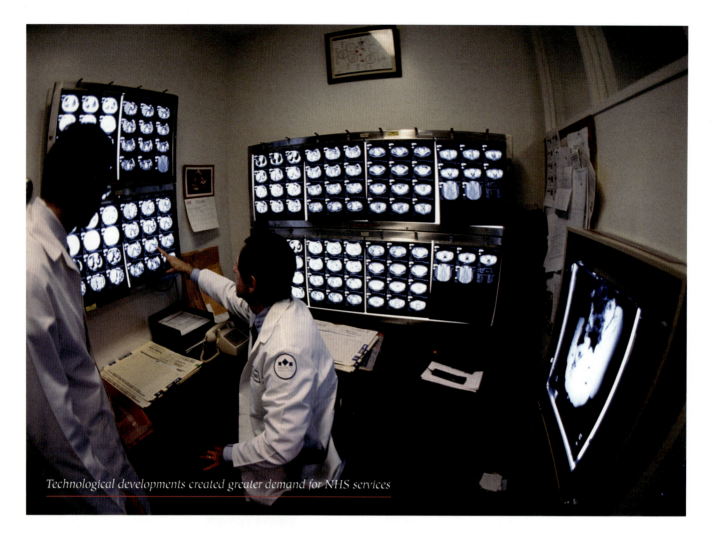

Technological developments created greater demand for NHS services

demonstration that the 'pool of illness' is never likely to diminish.

Improving health?

A much more realistic hope was that a national health service would produce a greater improvement in the health of the British people than would have occurred had the previous ramshackle system been allowed to continue.

While there have been many positive aspects of health experience in Britain since the creation of the NHS, there have also, unfortunately, been many negative aspects as well.

Even with regard to the improvements, it would be a mistake to attribute all of them solely to the existence of the NHS. Improved nutrition, housing and education are, arguably, equally powerful factors which influence the health of the population. As the 1979 Royal Commission on the NHS

admitted, how far improvements in health can be attributed to the NHS is "In one sense … quite impossible to answer because there is no way of knowing what would have happened if the NHS had not been introduced in 1948". Furthermore, improvements in health care have occurred in all developed countries, irrespective of how they have organised their health services, and indeed in some of these countries the improvements have been more impressive than in the UK.

Collective responsibility?

As was discussed in Chapter 6, the aim of Aneurin Bevan was to produce a national health system which was based on the principle of collective responsibility by the state. It could be said that this was achieved in 1948. After all, the very act of creating the NHS ensured that, collectively, the state assumed responsibility for providing a centrally organised system of health care.

Some critics have argued, however, that this principle was undermined during the Conservative years, 1979 – 1997. They argue that the Conservative government, which was committed to increasing the powers of market forces and to encouraging the growth of the private sector, seriously threatened the notion that there should be a collective interest in the provision of health care. The Labour government committed itself to the principles of the NHS and to increasing public spending.

Comprehensive and free?

It is generally agreed that the NHS provides a wide (or comprehensive) range of services for the care and treatment of the population for most conditions. Indeed, improvements in medical technology and in facilities generally have meant that, in many respects, services have become even more comprehensive.

Some people have argued in favour of changing the basis of the way we pay for our health services by moving away from the present system, which is basically funded from general taxation, towards one based on private or social insurance with the opportunity for individuals to opt into a private insurance scheme. While there are arguments to be made for alternative funding systems, taxation has remained as the principal source of funding. It is generally recognised that if tax funding was abandoned, the commitment to the principles of universality and comprehensiveness would be seriously compromised. (See pages 101–103.)

On the other hand, it can be claimed that the ideal of a 'free' service was conceded as early as 1951 when the Labour government introduced charges for dental work and spectacles. Successive governments have extended and increased these fees for NHS users. Nevertheless, some people have responded that, since charges for services have never contributed more than 6% to the total NHS budget, the principle, in practice, has not been dispensed with, only modified.

Equal access?

The aim of creating a uniform or equal standard of health care in terms of both quality and quantity for all citizens was always going to be a difficult objective to achieve. Part of the problem is that there are different interpretations of the term 'equal'. Equal can refer to an equal share of health care between individuals or between different groups of people or between different regions of the country.

With regard to one of these interpretations, the availability of services in different regions of the country, governments have achieved some success. In the

other aspects, however, equality has been more elusive. As we have seen, people continue to have different ease of access to health care, different qualities of health care available to them and different experiences of ill health. Despite the widely held belief that we have a *national* health service, access to treatment varies according to factors such as where people live, their gender and to which ethnic group or social class they belong. Furthermore, the so-called 'Cinderella' services for the mentally ill, those with learning difficulties and the elderly have always been under-resourced in comparison to the acute sector of care.

Public Opinion

One way of judging the NHS is to consider the views of the general public. A nationwide survey carried out prior to the 2005 general election makes interesting reading.(See Figure 10.4.) Despite record spending on the NHS, a significant number of people were dissatisfied. Only 29% were of the opinion that the NHS had improved, while over 40% stated that it had got worse. A staggering 60% were of the view that the extra money had been wasted. The only comfort for Labour was the public's view that Labour would provide better health care than the Conservatives.

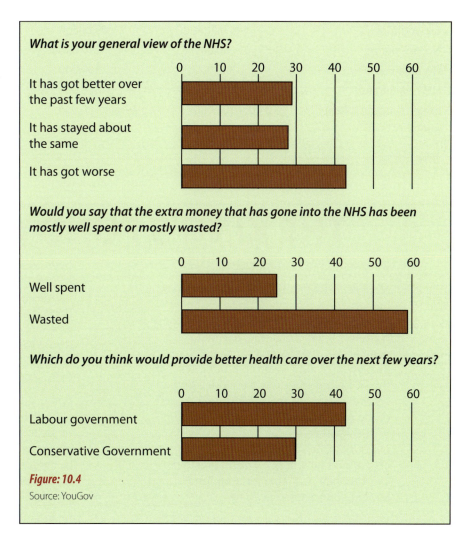

What is your general view of the NHS?

It has got better over the past few years

It has stayed about the same

It has got worse

Would you say that the extra money that has gone into the NHS has been mostly well spent or mostly wasted?

Well spent

Wasted

Which do you think would provide better health care over the next few years?

Labour government

Conservative Government

Figure: 10.4
Source: YouGov

The general health of the British public has improved in recent years—people are living longer and the death rates for cancer and coronary disease are decreasing. However, inequalities still remain as highlighted in Chapter 7. Furthermore, the 'affluent Western world diseases' such as obesity, and also drink-related deaths are increasing. The verdict has not changed that the NHS is a victim of its own success.

Table 10.5 provides a concise overview of Labour's stewardship of the NHS in England. (A similar picture would apply to Scotland.) An independent review of the NHS under Labour (1997–2005) by the King's Fund Audit (see below), concluded that huge strides have been made in reforming the NHS. However, while there is evidence of improvements in the nation's health, significant health inequalities still exist. Such a verdict seems harsh, especially when one compares the respective records of the NHS in Scotland and in England. (See page 111.)

NHS UNDER LABOUR (England and Wales)

	1997	2005
Staff	1.1 million	1.3 million
Expenditure	£44 billion	£68 billion
No. of Doctors	90,000	110,000
No. of Nurses	305,000	390,000
NHS waiting list	1,160,000	858,000
Breast cancer mortality	34 per 100,000	29 per 100,000
MRSA	389 deaths	5,000 deaths

Table 10.5 Source: *Sunday Times* 6.3.06

THE KING'S FUND AUDIT

The key findings of the audit were:

- ✍ NHS spending: Labour has met its spending targets thanks to an unprecedented increase in investment. Spending on the NHS in England has now reached European levels of expenditure. Nevertheless, questions remain over the productivity of the NHS and the value for money taxpayers are getting for their investment. Much of the additional new money for the NHS in 2006 will go on pay and other 'cost pressures' such as clinical negligence claims and new drugs. This means the extra money available for additional patient services is only 2.4%.

- ✍ Waiting times: Labour has made huge progress in the area which was its highest priority for the health service.

- ✍ Tackling big killer diseases: Labour has substantially met its targets to get more

beds, staff and equipment into services for treating cancer, heart disease and mental health. Mortality from cancer, heart disease and suicide has fallen, although these numbers were falling anyway. Progress on preventive measures, such as reducing smoking and improving diet, seems slow at best.

- ✍ Beds, staff, the private sector and MRSA: Labour has secured a substantial increase in some types of hospital beds and in clinical staff, and has made good progress in modernising NHS facilities. On the downside, rates of MRSA incidence compare badly with rates in other countries.

- ✍ NHS buildings: In 1997, the average age of NHS buildings was older than the NHS itself. By 2005, this was true of less than a quarter of NHS buildings. By 2010, 40% of NHS buildings will be less than fifteen years old.

SCOTLAND v ENGLAND

A May 2005 article in *The Herald* newspaper proclaimed

> "Sickly Scotland lagging behind care improvements south of the border."

The article presented some key evidence on how the neighbouring systems have performed since responsibility for health care was devolved. The article stated: "of the nine areas examined, it is apparent Scotland has made greater progress in one—the speed of treating patients with heart problems. On five criteria covering cancer treatment, waiting lists, and the queues in accident and emergency, it appears our service is lagging while England has been gaining ground or pulling away." (See NHS Report Card.)

Critics argue that Scotland's poor showing is due to its hesitancy over working in partnership with the private sector. The use of mobile private clinics in the UK to carry out routine operations has helped to reduce waiting lists. By January 2006, 130,000 people had used this type of treatment centre programme since it was launched. A lack of resources should not be blamed as Scotland has more doctors, more hospitals and more money spent per head of population.

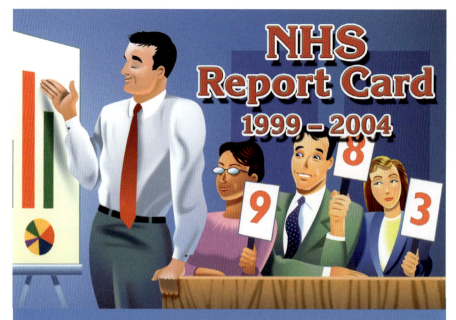

NHS Report Card 1999 – 2004

Waiting to see a consultant
In 1999 waiting times were higher in England than in Scotland
Verdict: By 2004 patients waited longer in Scotland

Waiting lists for operations
The number of patients waiting for an operation in Scotland increased by 17% between 1999 and 2004. In England the number decreased by 20% in the same period.
Verdict: Trend is falling in England but rising in Scotland

Workforce
Verdict: Numbers grew far faster in England than in Scotland

Long waits for hospital appointments
Verdict: Outpatients waiting more than six months to see a consultant was virtually eliminated in England. In Scotland 40,000 people were waiting more than six months to see a consultant by 2004.

Cancer Treatment
Verdict: English patients were treated earlier.

MRSA Infection
Verdict: Similar levels of infection were found in English and Scottish hospitals.

Heart Disease
Percentage of people waiting more than six months for angiographies was 3% in England. In Scotland all patients were seen within six months.
Verdict: Scotland ahead on heart operations.

Source: *The Herald* May 2005